The Motherhood Diaries 2

ReShonda Tate Billingsley

Houston, Texas * Washington, D.C.

This book is a work of fiction. Names, characters, places and incidents are products of the author's imagination or are used fictitiously. Any resemblance to actual events or locales or persons, living, dead, or somewhere in between, is entirely coincidental

Brown Girls Publishing, LLC
www.browngirlspublishing.com

ISBN: 978-1-6251745-2-9

First Brown Girls Publishing LLC trade printing
Cover designed by: Jessica Tilles

Manufactured and Printed in the United States of America

DEDICATION

For my mother...who warned me that payback wasn't pretty.

TABLE OF CONTENTS

Introduction ix

Diary of a Not-So-Super Mom

By ReShonda Tate Billingsley 1

Diary of a Naive Mom

By Denise Madre 20

Diary of a Disowned Mom

By Angela Aubrey 31

Diary of an Embarrassed Mom

By Tia McCollors 38

Diary of a Circus Mom

By Gina Johnson 48

Diary of a Mortified Mom

By Regina Cooper 58

Diary of a Grey-Haired Mother

By Edna Pittman 63

Diary of a Justabusymom

By Andrea Odom Campbell 72

Diary of a Big-Hearted Mom

By Latrice Martin 77

Diary of an Overwhelmed Mom

By Stephanie Bullock Ferguson 82

Diary of an Uninformed Mother

By Keria Burkhalter..89

Diary of a Map Maker's Daughter

By Nikki Woods 98

Diary of an Autism Mom

By Janoah White 107

Diary of a Mom Who Shoots From the Hip

By Deborah Gaffney..115

Diary of a Mother Raising Three Sons

By Patricia Markham Woodside...............................120

Diary of a Ninja Mom

By Denise A. Kelley..127

Diary of a Perfectionist Mom

By R. Ellen Crigler 133

Diary of a Smiling Mom

By Primrose Cameron 141

Diary of a Faithful Mother

By Naleighna Kai 147

Diary of a Mom Who Laughs A Lot

By Marcena Hooks...157

Diary of a Stepmother

By NiaShanta McClellan Ross 164

Diary of an Almost Teen Mom

By Kay Alizeti 174

Diary of a Modernized Mother

By Yolanda D. Gautier..181

Diary of a Reading Mom

By Kimyatta Walker 189

Diary of a Telecommuting Mom

By Kimberly Holley Clark...................................196

Diary of a Renaissance Mom

By Kristen Wright Matthews..............................203

INTRODUCTION

I've always believed that laughter is an awesome medicine. I just never knew motherhood would be one of the ways I kept my full dosage. But with kids like mine, who I often look at in awe and wonder where they came from, there is no shortage of laughter in my home. Between the fourteen-year-old and her dry wit, the eleven-year-old, with her corny humor (just like her mom), and the youngest, who at six, simply amazes us daily with the things that come out of his mouth, my family is forever laughing.

Since I always have been the journaling type (I started keeping a diary at age seven), it was only natural that I share some of those hilarious stories in written form. First, it was in a journal (which I plan to present to my children when they're grown), then, later, on social media.

One thing that social media taught me, was that my family wasn't alone. From my old school parenting style, to my rants about motherhood, I found a commonality with other mothers who shared similar experiences, recounted even worse thoughts, and provided encouraging words. And along the way, I also discovered moms just like me who made laughter a staple in their household—even if sometimes, they just had to laugh to keep from crying.

It was the feedback on social media that led me to writing the first *Motherhood Diaries*. In that book, I shared the good, the bad and the ugly of raising kids in the new millennium. Other mothers joined me as we talked about the triumphs and the tragedies, the hilarity and the heartbreak of raising children. It was a powerful collection of stories from women who showed other mothers that they are not alone.

The feedback from Book One was phenomenal, so much so, that we decided to do it again. But this time, we just wanted to focus on those humorous and heartwarming musings on raising kids. And the range of stories will once again unite mothers. There are tales of embarrassment, of laughter, of faith, and hope—we cover it all in *The Motherhood Diaries 2*.

Our hope is that you'll see something that's relatable (and ignore the stories that have you wanting to call Children's Protective Services). We hope you'll laugh and find both humor and solace in other mother's experiences.

Once again, I feel compelled to remind you that none of us in this book are child specialists, therapists, psychologists, or anything of the sort. Not legitimately anyway. But I think I'd be on target to say we all should have honorary PhD's in parenting, obtained through trial by fire. Technically speaking, though, we're just mothers who are trying to get this mothering thing down enough to produce wonderful kids.

Let me pause for this major disclaimer: Throughout this book, you may see words like "beat," "choke," and "stomp down." It's not literal. There are no child abusers here. Even when we snap. Even when we threaten to snatch out their urethra (or is that just me?) or "knock them into next week"—even during those times, we love our children. And they know it.

Are we clear on that? Good.

Now, if you're a perfect mother, whose kids keep their rooms clean, who never make you raise your voice, and who are perfect little angels, then good for you (good thing you can't see my eye roll right now). If you've never threatened bodily harm and have never had to repeat a request, we salute you. You can read on anyway and laugh at all us moms who aren't as lucky.

But if you're one of those mothers who sometimes takes the long way home, who has ever counted down to graduation, or who has ever had to remind herself that it's not nice to curse out your kids... then, lock the door, grab a glass of your favorite wine and see that you're not alone in these humorous and heartwarming musings on motherhood.

Enjoy,
ReShonda

The Motherhood Diaries 2

Diary of a Not-So-Super Mom

By ReShonda Tate Billingsley

Growing up, I used to always proclaim that I was going to be a Super Mom... able to change diapers in one swipe, whisk kids from one event to another in a single bound, provide loving, gentle discipline without ever raising my voice. I even wrote it in my diary at age fifteen.

October 12, 1985

Dear Diary, Love my mom, but I'm soooo gonna be a different type of parent. All that yelling and fussing she's always doing, that's not gonna be me. I'm going to be patient and kind—an awesome mom who is also best friends with my kids. My kids are gonna love me. Signed, Future Super Mom!!

I'm struggling to stifle my laugh right now. *(Ahhh, the innocence of childhood).* But yes, I had my Mother Plan all worked out. I had no doubt that I'd implement it. And I did, for the first twelve months of my oldest daughter's life. I baby-proofed everything, read every book and article on parenting, played Baby Mozart constantly, read stories to her in French to expand her vocabulary, and shuttled her to play dates. I was, indeed, Super Mom. And proud of it.

By daughter number two, the 'S' on my chest was getting a little tattered. Mozart was replaced by Mary J. Blige. French stories were replaced by Dr. Seuss and I made her play with her sister.

By the third child—my son—that 'S' was buried in the back closet somewhere. Now I was blaring Tupac and reading the National Enquirer.

Yes, three kids will definitely make you rework your life's plan. Especially *my* three children. Besides their hyper activeness, my children keep me on my toes because of their unbelievable sense of humor.

Laughter has always been a staple in my marriage. My husband and I both have moderate sense of humors that kept a spice in our life. We had no idea that having kids would take that to a whole other level. And it seems with each child that came along, the propensity for our house to become comedy central, escalated.

The ringleader of the Billingsley Comic View reality show would definitely have to be my six-year-old son, Myles. On any given day in my household, my son—who I'm convinced has been here before—will do or say something that will leave us in stitches.

Whether he's asking outrageous questions like "Do you have to eat hair when you're pregnant for your baby to have hair?" or summoning his imaginary Playboy status when he was bitten by fire ants, lay on the sofa like he was dying, and proclaimed, "Ma, if I don't make it, tell my girlfriend not to date another man." (Of course, I'm constantly trying to remind this little tyrant that he's too young to be thinking about girls. I get no help from my husband though; he gives his "little stud" a fist bump whenever he talks about girls. This is the same man that wanted to choke the poor little boy down the street for winking at his twelve-year-old daughter. Men!)

Girls really are the least of my worries with my son, though. It takes everything I have just to keep up with him. And his humor.

Take the time he walked in on me getting out the shower and fell to the floor, hands over his eyes, screaming, "My eyes! My eyes! Help me, Lord! My eyes are burning!!!"

I stood over him, naked as the day I was born, wondering if I should laugh, or tell him that's what his behind gets for not knocking.

Myles' social personality is going to be the death of me. He's done things such as planned a Super Bowl party on his own (he made invitations and passed them out to his friends, advertising a party from 12 pm to 12 am. He claimed he woke me up one morning at five to ask me could he have the party and I said 'yes'). Then, there's the time we went to the park. He met a kid and ten minutes later, came running over to me, "Mom, can my best friend..." He turned to the freckle-faced kid. "What's your name again?"

"Charlie," the little boy replied.

"Yeah," Myles said, turning back to me. "Can my best friend, Charlie, come over today and play?"

And, of course, I can't forget when some neighborhood kids rang my doorbell to see if Myles could come out to play. The problem with that is I have a gate around my house.

"Sweetie, how did you all get in the gate?" I asked, peering out at the closed gate.

The adorable little boy that rang the doorbell and who was obviously the spokesperson, shrugged his shoulders and said, "Oh, Myles gave the code to everybody on the bus so we can come over whenever we want."

Needless to say, I had to explain the purpose of the security gate and how he couldn't just go around passing out the code.

Myles is constantly doing things to make me question if he's been here before. Like this conversation:

"Mom, can I have $20. I'm broke."

"What happened to the money your grandpa gave you?" I asked.

"I got robbed," he replied.

I thought for a moment, then said, "Wait, didn't you spend that money at Game Stop on a new video game?"

Serious as triple bypass surgery, he looked at me and replied, "Yep, but with the prices they charge, it's like I said, I got robbed."

But just when I think my son is some kind of genius, he does things like call me disguising his voice.

"Hello," I said, answering the phone one afternoon when he called me.

"Yes, this message is for ReShonda Billingsley. I am calling to inform you that you won an all-expense paid trip to Disneyworld for you and your family. Please go ahead and buy your tickets now and come to the front gate and we will pay you back. Thank you."

Then, he hung up.

I wonder do things like Caller ID, or the fact that I gave birth to him and know his voice, register in his six-year-old mind?

Yes, just when we think he's Albert Einstein reincarnated, Myles reminds us that he's just a six-year-old boy. Like recently, he saw the Easter Bunny at the mall. He is afraid of costumed characters, so he announced, "Mom, I'm going over. I'm ready to face my fear."

He got up the nerve, went over and shook the Easter Bunny's hand, then came back to me and declared, "I did it! I'm ready to take on Chuck E. Cheese!"

Another reminder came when we were watching the second inauguration of President Barack Obama, and Myles decided to take the oath with the president. He said he was "practicing because one day I'm going to be president if I don't become a back-up dancer for Chris Brown."

Myles' humor is that kind of turn-your-head so he can't see you laughing, but all three of my children have taught me lessons through laughter. Let me share a few:

Be careful what you wish for

I teach my kids to be analytical thinkers. I wanted them to rationalize and think things through before forming an opinion. That's not always a good thing. In fact, it can lead to ineffective threats.

Case in point. The time I told my oldest, "If you don't get in here and do what I told you to do, I'm gonna bust your head to the white meat."

She just stared at me before saying, "Oh, my God, what does that even mean? And do you know anyone who has ever had that done to them? I mean, if I Google it, will I find pictures? Is that even legal?"

I could only sigh and leave the room.

My children even argue analytically. One day, I heard the two girls going at it because Morgan wore some of Mya's clothes (mind you, Mya is always in my stuff, but she doesn't want anyone touching her things).

"I'm not hurting your stupid clothes!" Morgan yelled.

"That's why you look like an abstract painting!" Mya countered, pointing to her sister's colorful outfit. "Like Picasso was really in the moment!"

An abstract painting? Picasso? That's your comeback? *Really?* (Memo to self: Make sure my kids stay in the suburbs because they wouldn't make it in the hood...)

Not to be outdone, even Myles tosses in his critical thinking. One time, Mya showed him a picture she took at the wax museum with Michael Jackson.

"I told you, Michael came back from the dead. That's really him," she said.

To which Myles replied, "You must think I'm stupid. That can't be real. If God said I can bring you back from the dead to take a picture with one person, I promise, MJ wouldn't have said you!"

Be careful what you say

My middle child, Morgan, is my hustler. She is forever looking for ways to make money. We'll go visit someone and next thing I know, she's scrubbing their toilet for five dollars.

Once, when I caught her doing that, I asked her what in the world was she doing.

"You told me I need a job," she said. "I'm working."

I had to explain that I didn't mean that *literally.*

"Oh," she replied. "Wish you would've explained that before I took all these pre-orders."

"Preorders?" I took the piece of paper that she'd extended toward me. Then, I saw it. A list of names and amount paid. My child had actually gone to school and taken preorders (WITH PAYMENT) for Blow Pops and Laffy Taffy!

One of the biggest areas where I had to learn to taper what I say is answering every request from my kids with the "No, you can't have that, I'm broke." (Hey, my kids subscribe to the 'you have not because you ask not' theory).

Well, unbeknownst to me, Myles decided to take his piggy bank to school one day and count out fifty pennies for lunch.

"Baby, have your mother send a check," the lunch lady told him.

I can only imagine the sad look on his face as he told her, "I can't. My mama is broke."

When he walked in that afternoon, relayed that story, then handed me the free lunch application the lunch lady had given him, I wanted to crawl under a rock. I could just hear those teachers in the teacher lounge talking about 'the book lady who can't buy her kid lunch.'

Learn how to work technology before using it

I've been married eighteen years, and I travel a lot, so I'm always on the road. One day, I decided to do something I had never done before—send sexy lingerie pictures to my husband. I'm talking, you would've thought I'd been watching the Playboy Channel, all these poses I was doing.

Having worked in the media for twenty years, I'm a little paranoid about some kid in Thailand getting his jollies because he's hacked into my phone and intercepted my dirty pics. So, I didn't send the raunchiest pics. But who needs to press send when you have iCloud? (for you non-Apple users, iCloud is like a storage in the sky). You can store your important documents, files and yes, pictures. And it even automatically backs everything up for you. Isn't that nice?

But somewhere in the owner's manual, I wish they had told me that all of my photos are automatically backed up and stored in the iCloud (or maybe they did tell me, but who reads all that stuff in the manual anyway?). Unfortunately, I found out about this back-up thing the hard way.

One day, while working in my office, my oldest walked in with my son. They had these horrified looks on their faces and I immediately panicked.

"What have you guys done now?"

My son stood there, speechless and I jumped into mommy discipline mode.

"What is it? Did you break the iPad?" I asked, since it was clutched tightly in front of my son's chest.

And then, Mya removed the iPad from his grip, and handed it to me. "You know we're traumatized for life, right?"

"What?" I said, taking the device. "What are you...." It was my turn to be speechless. There, in full screen, was my sexy photo. The raunchy one that I didn't get up the nerve to send. Apparently, ALL of my pictures had backed up from my phone to iCloud, and synced to every device connected to my Apple account—which would be all three of my children's iPads.

To say I was horrified would've been the understatement of the century. I'm sure this is where the experts would say I should've sat my children down and explained to them that sometimes mommies and daddies do adult things ... yada, yada, yada. But the only words I could utter were, "Go to your room!"

I couldn't look my kids in the face for a week after that.

Despite that, I am still more tech savvy than a lot of parents. I know that with ever-changing technology, I have to stay one step ahead of my kids when it comes to social media. But if I'm so tech savvy, why is it I keep "getting got" by the ol' voicemail message. You know the one. Morgan has it on her phone.

Me: (speaking after calling her) Hello.

Her: Hey.

Me: What are you doing?

Her: What? I can't hear you.

Me: I said, what are you doing?

Her: I can't hear you. Speak up.

Me: (screaming) I said what are you doing?

Her: What's wrong with your phone? I can't hear.

Me: (yelling like an idiot) What's wrong with your phone????

Her: Haha. I'm not in...leave me a message and I'll call you back!

And I fall for that over and over. It's the most irritating thing ever!

Stay faithful because they do take note

We are a faith-filled family. No, we don't go to church as much as we should (getting three kids ready for church, hearing them beg for donuts at the donut shop across the street from the church, the whole process is just simply exhausting)... but we are rooted in our faith.

My children sometimes remind me just how much. Take for example, a night out at dinner. Myles, who was five at the time, leaned over to the couple next to us and said, "Excuse me, do you believe in God?"

The elderly woman flashed a huge smile. "We sure do," she said.

"Oh, I was just wondering because you didn't say your grace," he replied.

I was so embarrassed but they just smiled and said, «You're right» before bowing their heads. I know they probably thought I was some kind of religious nut but I have no idea where he gets this stuff! (But he is seriously the grace police. Usually it's just to family, though).

Sometimes, my children's questions stump even me.

While driving one day, Myles asked me, "Mom, if Adam and Eve were the first man and woman and we're all descendants, wouldn't that make you and daddy related?"

"Ewww, that's nasty," Morgan chimed in.

Or this question. "Why do we have the groundhog determine whether we have six more weeks of winter? Why can't we ask someone like God or Jesus or Thor?"

And once again, both times, I had to go to my standard mommy answer. "Mommy's in a no talking zone, so since I don't want a ticket, I'll tell you later."

Even in church, Myles can be a character. One Sunday, the pastor asked for anyone having relationship problems to come to the altar. Myles stood.

"Where are you going?" I asked.

"You heard the pastor. To the altar. My girlfriends are stressing me out." *Did you notice that girlfriends was plural?* Of course, I made him sit his little behind down.

But hey, at least he knew who the pastor was. When Mya was hospitalized with pneumonia, our pastor and his team came to visit her. When they walked in, Mya, looked at him and said, "Are y'all from the state?"

The looks my minister gave me ranged from *If you had this baby in church more, she'd know who I was* to *So, does the state come visit you often?* Needless to say, that was one of my more embarrassing moments.

There's nothing like sibling love

Growing up, my sister and I never fought. I mean, never. That was mainly because she did whatever I told her (wish I still had that same pull), so I wasn't used to the constant bickering that came along with siblings.

And boy, do my kids bicker. I think that's what makes me snap the most, the constant arguing. The funny part is, ten minutes after a big blowout, they're all sleeping together in one bed, despite the fact that each has their own bed.

But they often bicker in pairs, and Myles is usually at the brunt of their torture. Like recently, my baby came to me and said, "Mom, why am I mistake?"

"What? Who told you that?" I asked.

"Morgan said I shoulda been a pool."

I sighed as I recalled explaining to my girls how we couldn't get a pool built because we had a baby boy on the way. I never knew they would later use that against him.

I side-eyed my daughters as he continued. "Mya said you cried, and wanted to throw yourself in front of a train when you found out about me."

Dang, those little eavesdropping trolls!

"Baby, those were tears of joy," I said soothingly.

It was Mya's turn to side-eye me. "But yet, *I* get in trouble for telling fibs."

Since I am a big proponent of truth-telling, my kids are quick to call me out when they think I'm being less than truthful.

Recently, Morgan tried out for cheerleader in her middle school. I really wanted to talk her out of it since she can't jump two inches off the ground or turn a cartwheel to save her life. But she was dedicated and committed and really wanted to do it, so I let her. Since most of the girls she was going up against had been cheering since they were eight months old (at least it seemed that way), of course, she didn't make the team. But she has the best attitude and said, "It's okay, mom. At least I tried my best."

That warmed my heart and I gave her a speech on how proud I was of her for trying.

"You are really good and probably would've made the team if they didn't have so many people trying out," I told her.

Mya looked at me, and shook her head and said, "You really should get mother of the year for that fable."

Then, Myles chimed in, "Yeah, because you know that girl sucked!"

The beauty in their battles, however, is they can mess with each other, but they won't stand for anyone else doing this. That's some kind of sibling love.

Orange isn't my color

Sometimes, I have to remember, I'm too pretty for prison. My fourteen-year-old, well, sometimes I have to laugh, to stay sane, or keep from snapping, or going to jail. Like many teens, she quite often, takes me there. Those of you with teens may know where *there* is. It's that abysmal place in between reality and fantasy, where otherwise sane women can lose all good sense and turn into a raging lunatic.

For me, *there* came one day at Mya's cheer competition.

"Mom, I want this picture package," she said, in her whiny, everything-is-about-me tone.

I shook my head. "No, Mya, that's $175 and the line is way too lo..."

I didn't get a chance to finish my sentence because this little thang, huffed, rolled her eyes, turned and stomped away.

I swear my world went black. *There* only takes a nanosecond to get to. And Mya had taken me in half a nanosecond.

Before I knew what I was doing, I reached up and snatched Mya by her ponytail, yanking her back toward me. Thank God my girlfriend was there to snap me back to reality or I would've been the focus of the viral video, "Crazy mom goes ballistic on daughter."

As my daughter's eyes bucked and my grip tightened on her ponytail, my friend stepped toward me and with a smile, whispered, "You're a public figure, a well-known author, you used to work for the news, you can't be *on* the news."

I inhaled. Exhaled. Then, slowly released my grip as I descended back into reality.

I've had other blackout moments as well. Like the time my son got in trouble for saying a curse word at school. He played dumb when I asked him, "What bad word did you say at school today?"

His brow furrowed as if he was in deep thought. "Monster? Alien? Stupid?"

"Boy, don't play me with me. Your teacher said you said 'shit'," I snapped.

He feigned confusion. "That's a cuss word? Some kids at my school said it before, so I didn't know. I am just six."

So I gave him the benefit of the doubt, along with a good scolding. When my husband came home later, he sat my son down to talk to him about saying a bad word at school. Even though he played dumb with me earlier, Myles confessed to using it and knowing it was a curse word.

I was dumbfounded and told him, "So you just looked me in my face and lied to me?"

With all seriousness, he replied, "Technically, I didn't look you in your face, remember?"

My first instinct was to snatch him up, but my husband's laughter brought me back to the situation at hand... and I actually found myself replaying our conversation and wondering, *Did he look me in the face?*

Of the three, my oldest makes me recite my 'too pretty for prison' mantra most. Since she wants to keep her eyeballs, she's managed to get the eye rolling under control, but between the attitude and the theatrics, I take deep slow breaths on a consistent basis.

On one incident, I had just returned from a book tour. As soon as my plane landed and I turned on my phone, I saw no less than TWENTY texts from my daughter.

OMG, MOM PICK UP!

MOM, PLZ ANSWER!!!

OMG, MOM, CALL ME!!!

MOMMMMM!

Each text was in all caps, which means it's major, right? Well, maybe if you were talking about someone else's kid. I could barely swipe my phone to get to her number, as all kinds of tragic images ran through my head.

My heart raced as I waited for her to pick up. "Mya! Baby, what's wrong?"

"Huh?" she calmly said.

"What's wrong? I see all these texts and missed calls."

"Oh, I was trying to see if you could bring me some cookies and cream ice cream on the way home."

I hung up so the people sitting next to me on the plane didn't hear me launch into a Tourette's episode.

I often threaten bodily harm to my children, but luckily, I've never had to use it. As Mya says, they may have moments of temporary insanity, but they're not crazy. Although one Saturday night, I thought she was. She walked into my bedroom, fully dressed and looking cute in a t-shirt and some cut-off jean shorts.

"Where are you going?" I asked.

"Out," she replied. "I'll be back when I get back."

"Okay, be careful," I told her as I went back to working on my laptop.

She stood and stared at me in shock. "Would that ever really work?"

I didn't look up from my laptop as I replied, "Not as long as I EVER have breath in my body."

She nodded. "I didn't think so. My friend just told her mom that."

"Your friend is going to get you drop-kicked in the throat."

"Did I say I was going out? I meant, I'm not going anywhere. I was just taking pictures of myself in my new t-shirt," she said, with a smile.

"That's what I thought," I replied.

My good enough is ... well, good enough

I don't try to kid myself. I'm not going to win any Mother of the Year Awards. I try to be a good mother. Most of the time, I succeed—but sometimes, well I just don't know. Sometimes I have to remind myself 'your children come first.' And sometimes, despite the reminder, I still don't want to be bothered.

Like the time, after an exhausting day, Mya lost her first basketball game in a huge blowout. My girls are so "extra" and this day would be no different. Once we got home, she proceeded to have a huge, major, overdramatic meltdown.

I tried giving the whole 'winning isn't everything' speech, but that just made her cry louder (she's such a drama queen). I know it's wrong but I kept looking at my watch thinking, *I hope you wrap this meltdown up in the next 30 minutes because Scandal is about to come on!*

Or the time my son asked for $224 for the school book fair. No, that's not a typo. $224. When I looked at him sideways, he said "What? I want a lot of books. As an author I'm sure you appreciate that."

I gave him $20 and said, "What I appreciate is the library..."

But for every callous remark I make, ask anyone and they'll tell you, I will turn Mama Bear on someone who messes with my babies. I work overtime to make sure they are safe and protected. I'm always watching, and (you new-age-wanna-be-your-kids-friend parents might need to look away), going through my kid's phone, email, computers, drawers. Yes, they deserve privacy. And when they get their own place, they can have it. Until then I'm the president and CEO of the nosey mom club and I have carte blanche to peruse all of their belongings.

Yes, sometimes, thought, I admit, I can go a bit overboard. Like the time Myles was playing on his DS.

"This stripper is off the chain!" he yelled.

I snatched the game. "Stripper? What stripper?" I demanded to know.

He looked at me like I was two shades of crazy and replied, "Umm, the Stripper that knocks down the Leggo blocks. That's his name because he strips blocks down. What did you think it was?"

I hesitated, then handed the game back. "Nothing son. Carry on."

I even let his "Mommies are so strange" comment slide. Partially, because it was true.

No, I know I won't ever be honored for my parenting skills. But I do my best. And I used to feel guilty about not being a Super Mom. But I've learned to let go of the guilt. It's okay that I buy my kid's birthday cupcakes instead of bake them. It's okay that I occasionally bribe my kids with gifts to make my guilt of traveling absences easier to take. I've come to terms that my good enough is good enough. I'm raising well-rounded, intelligent, and yes, hilarious children. No one ever has to give me an honor for that. I'm honored enough at who they are becoming.

And I can't wait until they have children of their own... because I have a feeling that funny gene will live on.

Diary of The Naïve Mom… (Or Everything I Didn't Know)

By Denise Leora Madre

Many words accurately describe me: Creative. Insightful. Passionate. Optimistic.

But the one I like least... and which most thoroughly applies, I'm afraid... is naïve.

In high school, I heard a story about Toni Braxton being "discovered" while pumping gas. As I also harbored deep-seated dreams of singing stardom, I believed such a thing would happen to me. Only in my early 20's did I discover—to my great shock and confusion—that this occurrence was not only highly improbable, but also a poor substitute for a life plan.

Just before Thanksgiving during my freshman year at Howard University, I was hustled out of two hundred dollars by two men who didn't trust the American banking system and needed me to prove its accessibility with a quick ATM transaction. When I later discovered their treachery, I was dumbfounded. After all, one of them claimed to be a pastor and wore a gold cross around his neck!

But my *preciousness*—let's try that word for a while, shall we?—is nowhere clearer than in my expectations of motherhood.

Point of fact: as my head-in-the-clouds mentality presented even in my youth, my brother David predicted I would build my adult home atop a lush grassy lot and use the foliage as a floor. My children would eat tree bark and drink rainwater from the hole in our roof we'd call a shower. I would fashion their clothes from nearby leaves and discipline them with spiritual timeouts involving the lotus position and quiet, remorseful chanting.

David is a special person.

My current abode has carpeted floors, and to the best of my knowledge, my children do not eat tree bark. Yet I'm not entirely sure my expectations of motherhood were any less fantastical. Though my oldest natural son will be seven this year, I am amazed how many times I grumble, "Man, someone really should do xyz.... Oh, right. *I'm* the mother. I guess that 'someone' is me. No, that someone is *I*. Motherhood is no excuse for sloppy grammar. Though I could argue that motherhood kills brain cells as I no longer remember what I was supposed to be doing..."

Per the children's handbook, I could blame my naïveté on my mother and her unbelievable amazingness. My father was incredible, too, but Mommy was the eighth wonder of my world. She worked full-time outside the home yet gave me the attention of a stay-at-home mom. I remember her smiling face at every school performance, her encouragement during every personal trial and academic test. And as far as I could see, her success was an effortless matter of intention and action.

Oh, and having a daughter who never gave her a moment's trouble.

smiles sweetly

So armed with this foolproof prototype, I entered the maternity ward, ready for a storybook life complete with birds singing me awake and lifting the corners of my bedspread as I busied myself with morning chores. My children would be attentive and obedient—never cranky—and would love clean and crumb-free living as much as I.

(Hey, like you didn't envision the same thing!)

To be clear, my official entrance into motherhood was unplanned. My husband, Horace, had five children ages six to twelve when we met—let's pause a moment to digest that—and we planned to live as a family. So I fully expected and was crazy-excited to embrace the stepmother role right away, Disney depictions be darned.

But with a new baby on the way to boot?

Not so much.

In the spirit of full disclosure, my first-born son's conception was more inevitable than immaculate. I won't get into specifics about our birth control method except to say it was a six-letter word which rhymed with "cupid." We had been engaged five months by then and were crunching numbers to afford a wedding and a home large enough for our big brood when Charlie (a euphemism for one's menstrual cycle invented by my late best friend for reasons I no longer remember) didn't show up for the first time ever. And though movies and sitcoms can poorly reflect reality, this time they got it right: the fear, disbelief, and outright mania gripping a female lead who gets pregnant at the worst possible time?

All too real.

My first elegant response to those winking pink lines was to drop the stick in Horace's hands and run screaming from the room. (I still apologize to him for that reaction.) Though I recovered enough to smile through phone calls to my immediate family, I was nonetheless convinced that I'd been the victim of an elaborate hoax. I would lie in bed, an idle hand on my flat stomach, thinking, "They're all mistaken. Any day now, Charlie will come, and everyone will blame the positive test results on some bad leftovers...which reminds me: I need to clean out my fridge." It's not that I didn't want to be a mother; I just didn't believe he was real.

Rather, I should say "she," for I always believed my first-born would be a girl. I had no proof or particular reason, just a long-held wish, which matured into a fact. So after hearing my baby's heartbeat the first time, I began talking, quoting scripture, and singing to her, wanting my daughter to know my voice and associate it with something other than the total freak-out she heard when I learned I was pregnant. She endured several name changes before Horace and I happily landed on Braylee, a combination of our beloved grandmothers' names. As she bloomed in my belly, I could not wait to meet her and put those many years of Cabbage Patch Kid care to use.

So imagine my reaction during the second ultrasound when the technician wondered aloud why Horace and I kept referring to the baby as female. I replied with confidence, we believed we were having a girl. She nodded, punched a few buttons on the machine, and turned the monitor our way with a grinning, "Oh, because you're wrong!"

And there was the smoking penis.

(Not literally because that would be wrong and terrifying, but you get what I'm saying.)

Well. I don't know what ol' girl expected me to do, but I went into hysterics. I cried and shook my head chanting, "No, no, no!" and "She took my daughter! Why would she do that? Where's Braylee?" Fearing my sudden and acute distress would prevent her from continuing the ultrasound, the technician looked to Horace to calm me down. And though his imposing size and no-nonsense demeanor could be, uh, intimidating, Horace sided with the mouthy technician this time.

For he was as confused by my outburst as she.

And see, when I tell stories like this one, I feel the need to explain—no, to insist—that I'm not an emotional nutbag. I just expect things to go a certain way, and when they don't, I don't always handle the disappointment very well.

So maybe I'm not naïve... just immature.

Ouch.

Let's go back to naïve, okay?

So Braylee became Jonan, and I delivered my perfect little boy in April 2007. The memory still brings tears to my eyes. I didn't know that I could love someone so much or that my heart could swell without breaking. I loved my husband and his five children, but this precious angel was flesh of my flesh, someone who started as an infinitesimal blip on my radar and forever changed my name to *Mother.*

And I had no idea what that would entail.

Let's go back to my stepchildren. We got along like peas and carrots during their few visits while Horace and I were dating, and they seemed to like me. But despite my best intentions, our first several months together were not what I had expected—and not in a good way. There was tension, confusion, and silence so off-putting I sometimes felt like an unwelcome visitor in our home. I was dumbfounded by the awkwardness.

Yes, I was pregnant with Jonan and had hyperemesis (eleven letters spelling constant nausea, dehydration, and crankiness for any woman lucky enough to have it). And no, I had never lived with anyone besides my parents and brother—nope, not even at Howard—so I wasn't used to dealing with other people's messes and moods. But my naïveté outranks those contributing factors by a wide margin.

I didn't understand, or in any way anticipate, the challenges inherent in blending families, challenges the average person would likely see coming. Unconsciously viewing Horace's love and acceptance as a reflection of theirs, I thought our relationships would be seamless. And as I prepared for our cohabitation, I never considered their possible adjustment issues because I was too busy envisioning game nights in the family room and smiling faces singing carols around the Christmas tree.

There are worse ways to prepare for stepmotherhood, right?

My cluelessness with Jonan was different but no less significant. During his first three months of life, he woke himself up for nightly nursing. So when he began sleeping without interruption, I thought it was normal. He's a baby, but also a person. He knows when he's hungry and would awaken to tell me so, right? In the morning, when Horace would ask how Jonan fared overnight, I'd beam, "He did great!" Parents complained all the time about sleepless infants, and my son figured it out on his own in the first three months.

Score!

Jonan was missing two meals per night then thought it would be fun to reject one of my breasts. It must have been the left, for it still seems rather sad about it. Pumping was a disappointing, time-sucking endeavor yielding a paltry three ounces at best, but I once again figured, "If he were hungry, he'd eat. Or drink, as he's nursing. Hmmm, if the liquid constitutes a meal, does that make it eating?" So color me stunned during his next pediatric appointment when his doctor reported Jonan's weight loss and referred him to a growth specialist.

I really didn't see that coming. I feel foolish for saying it, but it's true.

Once Braylee arrived two years later, opportunities for my doe-eyed view of the world to be dismantled by reality multiplied exponentially. This paradigm shift goes beyond realizing I would never again use the bathroom, enjoy a meal, or make a phone call without interruption and beyond abandoning the hope that potty training would be simple, or that spending an afternoon at the playground would exhaust them, not me.

I was honestly surprised when reading my children a bedtime story resulted not in fluttering lashes and the softly pursed lips of slumber but energetic appeals for more stories. Confusion abounded when they would jump on the bed, stick toys in the VCR, and kick the wall with their inexplicably heavy feet as soon as I closed the door... and continue to do so after I specifically told them not to.

(Gasp!)

To top it all off, I didn't know that my becoming a mother would so greatly amuse my own saintly mother. Though we have talked and laughed about my childhood over the years, the arrival of my children unlocked a secret vault in her memory full of never-before-heard anecdotes starring yours truly as the mischievous, often destructive protagonist.

Me: So we had to take down Braylee's princess castle because she and Jonan turned it into a steel cage for their wrestling matches. Oh, and she pulled out one of the stabilizing rods and used it as a weapon. I don't get it. David and I had a sliding board in the living room as kids, and we...

Her: Destroyed it.

Me: (pause) We did? No, we used to…

Her: Do everything on that thing but slide: stomp, jump, bang, roll. It was up for two weeks before we finally got rid of it, afraid you were going to kill yourselves.

Funny. I don't remember it that way.

Me: You wouldn't believe how Braylee is eating her spaghetti. She's pulling out noodles one at a time and twirling them above her head.

Her: That's nothing. You used to grab fistfuls of mashed potatoes, squeeze them in your palm, and eat whatever came up through your fingers. And you were older than she is.

Me: (stomach churns)

Her: And let's not forget when you decided to eat like Cookie Monster until I told you he had poor table manners. (chuckles) There were crumbs and food flying everywhere…

Clearly I obtained my imagination and ability to spin a good yarn from her.

And while we're on the subject, I also didn't know the rules and standards Mommy applied to my childhood—the very ones which shaped the woman you read before you—would make her sigh disapprovingly when used on my children. Who knew that my mother's grandchildren were always well-intended, never naughty, and perpetually misunderstood?

(Insert long eye-roll here.)

"Oh, I know Jonan snuck into your bedroom, ate your cookies, and had the audacity to dunk them in your milk, but don't send him to bed early. They're only cookies, right?"

"And no, the boys didn't put the food away or clean the kitchen last night because they were too busy playing video games. And yes, this is the third night this week. But go easy on them. Being a teenager is hard."

I think she has selective senility. Or she enjoys watching me get as good as I (apparently) gave.

My mother's musings aside, perhaps my naiveté is a blessing. Without my pseudo-Pollyanna perspective, would I not have been afraid to withdraw from college twice, possibly never to return? Would I not have balked at going from zero to five children in the span of "I do"? Would I not have lacked the courage for a half-dozen other seemingly insane decisions if I had only known better?

Moreover, wouldn't life become pedestrian without a manageable margin of ignorance? Does not the gift of not knowing yield the possibility of constant wonder?

Sometimes I look at my children and marvel at how much they have shown me. Building relationships with my oldest five taught me to examine my motives, to measure my words and to treasure theirs. Despite the lack of biological connection, I see myself more clearly every time I look at them, to say nothing of Jonan and Braylee who are so much like me I feel I owe them an apology. I didn't know they could be so *me* and so *not me* at the same time... or that I could love all seven of them this fully and never feel as if I've reached my limit.

And if this is what being naïve gets me, I'll take it. Oh, and a handful of gold from the end of the rainbow where the unicorns roam.

Denise is a Gladiator in a Suit who was once referred to as "the black Elle Woods." The fictional characters she creates are real, and they're spectacular. Join her for grammatically-correct merriment at http://denisegettingtoyes.blogspot.com.

Diary of a Disowned Mom

By Angela Aubrey

I'm going to be honest. Motherhood made me hate my in-laws.

For two years, though, I adored them. And they, me. I fit right in to their rambunctious, unconventional family. Or maybe they were conventional, because like many people, they had the drunk uncle, the bible toting, quoting aunt, the loud-mouth cousins and the promiscuous sister. Every family gathering (and there were plenty) was bound to end with someone getting into a big argument. But again, I blended in because even though our backgrounds were vastly different, my husband and I were both outgoing people. And despite all the dysfunction, I really enjoyed my husband's family.

That is until my first child came along.

I had prayed for this baby and as a college educated woman, read everything I could, taken parenting classes, everything to properly bring this child into the world. I dissected information, analyzed and strategized to ensure that I was prepared.

So, when my mother-in-law held a piece of thread and a needle over my belly and declared that I was having a girl because it swung around and around in circles, I chuckled and blew her off. I was waiting to find out what I was having so I took her bootleg prediction with a grain of salt.

She showed up at my house the next day with a bunch of girl's clothes.

"We were waiting to find out the sex of the baby, remember?" I told her.

"Oh, no need to wait. The needle said you were having a girl," she replied like she'd just done a 4D ultrasound.

My husband gave me the 'just go with it' look, and so I did.

And then, a couple of days later, we sat in the kitchen as she told her sister (the bible quoting one), "When Eula Mae gets here..."

I stopped cooking, looked around and said, "Who is Eula Mae?"

The look on my face must've tickled Aunt Sue because she said, "Your baby." She laughed. "I still cant believe you're gonna let them name that baby, Eula."

"Ah, no," I replied. "I'm not."

My mother-in-law's eyebrows shot up. "But Brian said..."

"Are you crazy?" I shot in my husband's direction. By this point he was hiding behind a newspaper in the adjoining family room. "Why would you tell your mother that? You know I'm not naming my baby Eula Mae."

As if she were on stage in some dramatic performance, his mother's bottom lip quivered and she said, "That's my grandmother's name." To this day, I don't know how she got her voice to crack on cue.

I side-eyed my husband, who suddenly developed an extreme cough and had to exit the room. But there would be no 'just going with it' this time. I was not about to let this woman believe that there was a chance in hell I'd name my precious baby, if it was a girl, Eula Mae. We needed to nip that in the bud right now.

"I'm sorry, but if I have a girl, I'm going to name her McKenzie."

"McKenzie?" his aunt said, turning her nose up like she'd smelled something foul. "You gonna give that baby that white name?"

I inhaled, reminding myself that my mother had raised me better than to cuss out old people. "In case you forgot, I'm half white," I told her.

"Girl, look at that hair, you black," his aunt proclaimed, pointing to my bushy, curly fro.

That was the beginning of the end of my once-perfect relationship with my in-laws. His mother had an attitude with me after that. My husband had even tried to convince me to give the baby the middle name of Eula Mae, but since he really didn't care and was only doing it to keep the peace, I stood my ground.

Thankfully, a few months later when my *son* made his entrance into the world, it became a non-issue.

I thought things would get better, but they only got worse. We named my son after his father, Brian, *the second.* Of course, his family rolled their eyes and determined, he was Brian, *Jr.*

That, I "went with." But I couldn't get with it when a few weeks later, my mother-in-law called and asked, "How's my little Dookey?"

Yes, you read right. Dookey.

The first time I heard it, I thought she was just kidding around. Then, other family members started calling him Dookey (he did make loud noises when he had bowel movements, but my son would NOT be saddled with the nickname, Dookey).

So, when my sister-in-law picked him up, and tossed him in the air, I was ready to blow a gasket. (No, for real. She tossed him. Like, let him go and everything. It took everything in my power not to smack her, but she caught him, and even though my heart had dropped into the pit of my stomach, I 'just went with it.')

"Hey, Dookey!" she cooed.

I took a deep breath. "Please don't call him that. His name is Brian," I said.

"Oh, here you go," she sneered, before launching into a tirade about how uppity I was.

Needless to say, that visit didn't end well. Neither did several more after that, including one when my baby was six months old. My mother-in-law actually chewed up her steak, took it out her mouth, and gave it to my son (I screamed and snatched my son away before I realized it). She was insulted (I don't chew up my baby's food, so why in the world she thought it was okay that she did, was beyond me). We argued about everything— from her feeding him expired baby food (because "those dates don't really mean anything anyway"), to her completely disregarding my nap schedule to her brother putting my two-year-old son, and four other kids on the back of his pickup truck and driving them to the store.

Everyone said I overreacted because after all, they'd all done all the things I was horrified about, and no one had lost a kid yet. That was fine and dandy, but I didn't want my kid to be the first.

My own mother had passed when I was a teenager and the few relatives I had respected my boundaries when it came to my son. My husband's family didn't know what boundaries were.

It soon came to a point where I dreaded having my in-laws around. My husband, bless his heart, was very laid back and hated being in the middle. He tried countless times to talk to his family but no one paid him any attention. (I tried to get him to move us to Alaska and not leave a forwarding address. He wouldn't go for that, though.)

Finally, after watching my brother-in-law give my three-year-old a jalapeno pepper, then videotaping him as he freaked out, I decided enough was enough. The mama bear in me snapped.

"You're all crazy! Every one of you!" I screamed, silencing the room. "And if you want to be around my son, you will follow my rules!"

"Hmph, I see who wears the pants in this marriage," Uncle June muttered.

"So, you're one of those new age feminists," his aunt chimed in.

I don't proclaim to be new-age anything, and in fact, I do subscribe to the 'let the man lead' theory, except when it comes to my baby. I'm sure there's no caveat in the Bible, but it is what it is. My husband has taken a hands-off approach with his family, so mama has to be hands on.

Things tapered off a bit... but soon, returned right back to the way they were—his family overstepping boundaries when it came to my son.

But the straw that broke this mama's back came one Sunday afternoon, when my husband's Uncle June brought his pit bull to our house for my husband to keep while he went out of town for a week. The family was pretty upset with me because I adamantly refused that. I had to hear the "pits get a bad rap" speech, and how "Killer really wasn't a killer." But I didn't budge. I mean, they kept this dog tied to a tree in the back yard, so it was bound to snap at any moment. I slammed the door on Uncle June and his pit and essentially, my relationship with my in-laws.

I declared that little Brian would only see my dysfunctional in-laws with supervised visitation. That's what got me disowned. None of the family spoke to me for four months.

That was probably the most peaceful time of my life, but still for my husband's sake and because I know he loves his family, I did try to compromise and make peace when Brian turned five.

I acquiesced on the nickname (Dookey became Mookey), and I occasionally let them feed him cereal for dinner. I try not to be so high-strung because my mother-in-law was right, she had six kids and hadn't lost one (well, unless you counted Ricky, who was doing twenty to life for armed robbery). I don't know if it was because my son was older, but I finally came to terms with my in-law's ways. I pick and choose my battles and so far, we've found a happy medium.

But I think that's about to change. I just found out I'm expecting baby number two and if my mother-in-law heads toward me with that needle and thread...well, I can't make any promises.

Angela Aubrey is a freelance journalist in Dallas, Texas, where she lives with her husband and two children, a boy, and a girl (which her mother-in-law's needle accurately predicted).

Diary of an Embarrassed Mother

By Tia McCollors

Out of the Mouths of Babes

It happens to the best of us…and at the worst of times. It's the thing that we have the least amount of control over, but the thing that needs the most control. Yes, mothers. I'm talking about our children's mouths. There was a time that I thought I wasn't an easy person to embarrass, partly because I was quick-witted. But then I had children and I learned that physical traits like almond-shaped eyes, high cheek bones, and long fingers aren't the only things that our children inherit.

At forty, I've now (almost) mastered the art of keeping my comments to myself. At least most of the time. My thoughts still have the tendency to raid my face and show what I'm thinking, but I doubt that will ever be resolved. That's why I've turned my attention to teaching my children the art of subtlety and instilling in them the words that were often said to me: "You don't have to say everything that you're thinking." Sometimes they get it, and sometimes they don't. In the meantime, I've been learning to find golden nuggets of wisdom out of the mouth of my babes.

Learn to love every part of you.

Grocery store check-out lines give me the chills. My children seem to have the most thoughtful moments when I'm focused on unloading a shopping cart full of cereal, organic macaroni, boneless skinless chicken breasts, and boxes of pouched snack juices. I often try to distract them by giving them tasks like helping me to stack the yogurt, but their eyes are usually zeroed in on two people. The grocery store clerk and the bagger.

I won't even tell you about the time my daughter (who was three at the time), repeatedly asked me, "Is that a man or a woman? It looks like a man, but it sounds like a woman." Truth be told, I couldn't answer if I wanted to because I had no idea. But on another particular occasion I could tell something was about to go down. I was unloading my shopping cart when out of nowhere, a new bagger appeared. He looked to be in his late teens and his face was covered with more freckles that I'd ever seen. I practically threw the eggs and the milk on the conveyer belt, but it was too late. My daughter's eyes had already locked in on her target. She smiled at the bagger. He smiled at her. *This is bad*, I was thinking to myself. *The poor boy doesn't realize he's setting himself up*.

Then her words came. "You have a whole lot of polka dots of your face. You can play connect-the-dots anytime you want to."

He laughed in amusement and said, "Yep."

I breathed a sigh of relief and chuckled, too. The teenager had embraced his uniqueness and learned to love what God had given him. So what if we have skinny legs, thick thighs or if we're a little puffy under the eyes? Who is it to say that our feet are too flat, our lips too large, or breasts too small, or our shoulders too broad for a woman? Maybe it's been four years and you've yet to lose your pregnancy pouch. You aren't the only one, dear sister. Learn to love every little (or big!) part of you.

Get your information from a credible source.

The forecast called for a hot, muggy day with a high pollen count and I would've rather been at home tackling my never-ending to do list. But this always-involved mother had agreed to be a parent chaperone for my son's kindergarten trip to the dairy farm. By eight-thirty in the morning, the school bus was jostling and bouncing down the interstate for a forty-minute ride past downtown Atlanta and to this little corner of the country side.

After the gas fumes settled and the teachers calmed the excited students, we unloaded the bus and headed for the waiting trucks and trailers that were going to pull us around the farm for a hay ride. Straw flew into my mouth, hair and eyes, but seeing the thrill in my son's eyes made it worth it. At least that's what I told myself.

Afterward, we headed to the cow milking demonstration. Poor little Bessie's utters were hooked to a monstrosity of a machine while the dairy farm worker explained the process. My son was quiet. He's never quiet. Afterward, he passed on the offer for a glass of fresh milk, as did I. But for different reasons. Lactose is not this mommy's friend.

The next morning during breakfast, I offered my son and daughter a glass of milk to eat with their bacon and pancakes. My son looked at me in disgust and waved his hands in the air. "Oh, no," he said. He leaned across the table and told his sister, "I wouldn't drink that if I were you. That came from a cow's penis." It was nearly a month before the repulsion wore off and my children drank milk again.

I, on the other hand, gleaned something from my son's statement. Don't believe everything you hear. There are times when you need to research things for yourself, or at least find a credible source to validate the claims. Just because it's posted on the internet, distributed through social media networks, or whispered to you at the family reunion, doesn't mean it's true!

You have options.

Every year since the age of one, my children have had a themed birthday party. I admit, I like planning their parties as much as they like having them. Sesame Street, It's a Jungle Out There, Party Like A Rock Star, Gymnastics Girl,

Hoop It Up....I've done it all. But as my son approached his eighth birthday, I made a decision. He wouldn't have another birthday party until he hit the double digits. I'd take cupcakes to his classroom, then we'd have a low-key family celebration with his favorite meal and perhaps catch a movie. This was a change, and one that he wasn't used to. As his big day approached, his grandmother decided to ask him what he wanted for his birthday.

"A girlfriend," he said without a second thought.

"You need to think of something else," his grandmother advised him.

My son disappeared upstairs, returning about twenty-minutes later. "If I can't have a girlfriend, then I'll take a flat screen television," he announced.

Needless to say, he didn't receive either one but I admired his confidence for asking. Lesson number one: You have not because you ask not. Even if the answer is 'no,' it may be because you're not mature enough for what you're asking for. Lesson number two: Keep your options open. If the first, second, or third opportunity doesn't work out in your favor, keep working until you find something that does.

Be You.

My children are terrified of costumed characters. After visiting Disney World for four years in a row, you'd think they'd grow accustomed to oversized mice, ducks, and chipmunks wearing clothes, singing and dancing. I mean, who doesn't love Mickey Mouse and Pinocchio? My children do.....but from a distance.

I've been told they'd eventually outgrow their fears, but I've still done everything to try and allay their anxieties.

My son is the absolute worst. For the longest time he wouldn't even put a mask on his own face! One particular year he begged to dress up as Buzz Lightyear for Halloween. He stepped into the costume, pumped his fist toward the sky and yelled, "To infinity, and beyond." But everyone knows that Buzz Lightyear isn't complete without his space range helmet. However, my son refused to put on anything that covered his face. When I picked up the combination mask-helmet, he bolted into his sister's room and locked the door. But every mother knows the trick to opening locked bedroom doors.

Click.

Even though my son screeched at the top of his lungs, that didn't stop me from wrestling him down, sitting on top of him, and forcing the mask on his face. Evoking my own super powers, I somehow managed to pin his arms down so that he couldn't rip the mask off, then I carried him to the bathroom mirror.

With all of the thumping, bumping and screaming, it's a wonder that my neighbors didn't call Child Protective Services. I pressed ahead on my mission anyway. My son's head was buried in the crook of my neck.

"I don't want to turn into Buzz," he cried.

"Baby." I consoled him and lowered my voice to nearly a whisper. "You're not going to turn into Buzz. It's just a costume. Please trust, Mommy."

We both took deep breaths as he turned to examine himself. He tilted his head. He hesitantly touched the mask. He pulled it up to see his cute, brown face was still there. He put it back on. "I'm still me."

"I told you," I said, setting his feet firmly on the floor.

Suddenly, he ripped the mask off and zoomed away to play with his sister who had watched the entire fiasco wearing a tutu, fairy wings, and high-heeled princess shoes.

"I'm still not wearing that thing," he yelled over his shoulder.

The moral of this story? Don't let people turn you into something you don't want to be. Strip off your mask and let your real light shine!

Face Your Giant

The line at the post office snaked out of the front door but I didn't have time to return later. It seemed everyone in the city had a package to mail during their lunch hour. The only voices buzzing were those of the postal clerks. "Do you need stamps today?" "Would you like insurance on this package?" "Do you need to send this certified?" "You don't have enough postage." The rest of their patrons had their heads buried in their smart phones or seemed to be lost in thought.

It was close to my children's nap time so they were uncharacteristically calm. All was well. That is, until a six-foot-six bear of a man entered wearing jeans, leather boots, a leather vest and a neon orange bandana tied around his head. He had a line of earrings from the top of each ear and down to the lobe. I turned my body to shield my daughter's line of vision. She leaned to the right. I shifted. She leaned to the left. I turned, too. Before I knew it she deflected my moves and pushed around my defensive line.

My baby girl—all of three years old—short and stature but tall in boldness, put her hands on non-existent hips. She looked up into the eyes of the giant before her and said, "Boys don't wear earrings." Her voice echoed in the building.

Everyone's head whipped in our direction and we turned into the lunchtime entertainment. They were amused, but I dared not turn my head to see the full scale of this bear-man's reaction.

"Sorry," I apologized and pushed my daughter back in front of me. As soon as my transaction was over I scurried out of the front door. My little ones weren't the only ones who needed a nap. I wondered what my husband would say about his little princess this time. As usual, he'd probably think she was hilarious.

By the time I'd given my snack a crew and buckled them in, I heard a tap on the window. I turned to see the bear-man towering over my car. I let down the window just enough to hear his voice, but not enough for him reach in his paws to wrap around my neck.

He leaned down to talk through the crack. "I've been thinking about getting rid of these earrings for a long time.

Today's going to be my last day wearing them. I'm too old, now."

I breathed a sigh of relief. We'd all live to see yet another day.

"Thank you, baby girl," he said. He walked away, revved up his Harley Davidson motorcycle and sped down the street.

"I told you, Mommy," my daughter said, already drowsy. She sucked up the rest of the juice, handed me her trash, and let her eyes float closed.

She'd faced her giant. Like we all should. Oftentimes the thing that looks most intimidating, isn't as tough to tackle as we thought. We'll all be faced with situations where we'll be nudged to speak our minds or stand up for what we believe is morally correct. After all, we are our sister's keepers.

My son and daughter are growing and maturing. Now with another baby brother to influence, my life will continue to be filled with stories that I'll share with their spouses. Like my oldest children, their baby brother will probably shove fruit snacks up his nose, embarrass his parents, and unknowingly insult unsuspecting victims. As always, I'll hush him. But in the back of my mind, I'm still listening for the lesson.

Tia McCollors is the author of a growing number of faith-based novels geared toward women, as well as the non-fiction Prissy Purse Devotions series. She loves to share the laughable and embarrassing moments of her children. Tia lives with her family in the Atlanta, GA area. Find out more about Tia at www.TiaMcCollors.com or by visiting her Facebook fan page at www.Facebook.com/FansOfTia.

Diary of a Circus Mom

By Gina Johnson

I have always wanted to be a mother. From the time that I was six and carried my Cabbage Patch Kid around on my hip, I just knew—I was destined for motherhood.

I always imagined myself baking cookies with my children, having fun with them at the park, and gently cradling them in my arms as I rocked them to sleep. I was going to be the best mom in the world and I was going to have the best children in the world. Little angels.

But there were things about motherhood that no one told me. Dreadful, horrifying and hilarious things that I have come to learn. If you're reading this and you don't have children, take notes. This information will help you. If you're reading this and you already have children, I want you to know that it's completely acceptable for you to shout "Amen" while reading this. You will understand. And if you have children but can't relate to any of this... then, congratulations!

You have perfect children and are a perfect mother! You're probably also a robot, but I digress.

I'm going to be brutally honest about what motherhood has been like for me, the mother of three beautifully crazy children, who remind me of a circus.

Here are some things that I never knew about motherhood.

Number One: Your body will never be the same.

Now I'm sure some of you will say that you are one of those magical (read evil) women who fit right back into your jeans when you returned home from the hospital after giving birth. If you are one of those women, let me give you a piece of advice. Don't tell a lot of women that. I know it may be hard not to brag about it, but trust me on this one, I'm saving your life. Every time you brag about your flat stomach, you're tempting the mothers with not-so-flat stomachs to do you bodily harm. You don't want that. And neither do us moms with not-so-flat stomachs, but when we hear you talk about it, it's hard not to picture ourselves accidentally pushing you down a flight of stairs. There, I said it. You've been warned, so govern yourselves accordingly.

Now that I've gotten that out of the way, let me keep it real. I didn't have a flat stomach before having children. Sure, I love to blame all of my fluffiness on my children, but the truth of the matter is, I wasn't in perfect shape before the children arrived. For all of you who know me, savor this confession, because I'll never be this honest again.

But back to the subject at hand. Even though my body was less than perfect before becoming a mother, it somehow got worse. Much worse. My legs are different, my feet are different, my face is different and of course, my stomach has now become an entity of its own. Before becoming a mother I did sit-ups with ease. If I wanted to wear something that was form-fitting I could put on a pair of Spanx, and voila! Problem solved. Now, ten years after becoming a mother, I no longer do sit-ups with ease. Sit-ups involve determination, concentration and prayer. Determination to finish, because about halfway into the first sit-up I'm ready to quit life and just become a fat angel who enjoys all of the perks of Heaven like milk and honey. I'll bet food in Heaven is so good, but I digress. I need concentration while doing sit-ups because it's hard to ignore the laughter. Whose laughter? My stomach's. That's right. Every time I attempt to do sit-ups, my stomach laughs at me. Hard. And not just a giggle. A deep loud thunderous laugh that reminds me of my stomach's plan to take over my entire body, my entire life and eventually, the whole world. Don't try to figure it out. It's complicated.

Lastly, for me, doing sit-ups requires prayer because sometimes as I'm straining to finish. I see Jesus. Okay, not really, but at times it certainly feels like it has happened, or is about to happen. So during those intense moments all I can do is shout to the heavens for deliverance and, trust me, it works.

Number two: Your children will do bizarre things that will cause others to doubt your morals and your entire outlook on life.

If you're anything like me, you try to teach your children what's appropriate and what's not appropriate. You work hard to instill values into them that will make them polite children, and good citizens. If your children are anything like my circus, they will somehow always manage to do that one thing that makes it look like you've allowed them to run free in a barn from the time they entered the world.

My daughter is ten now and has pretty much mastered knowing the importance of one's personal space, but that wasn't always the case. Several years ago, we were at a graduation open house and were enjoying a friendly conversation with the father of an old classmate. For privacy purposes I'll refer to that poor man as Mr. Thomas. Mr. Thomas was smitten with Cierra as he talked about his desire to have grandchildren one day. Cierra giggled as he lifted her into the air and then held her as we finished our conversation. I was so engrossed with the conversation that I had taken my eyes off of Cierra. Everything was going well until I noticed Mr. Thomas' facial expression drastically change. In two seconds flat, the color of his face morphed from tan to crimson as he began attempting to put Cierra down. That's when I noticed it. My husband's daughter (because you don't claim your children when they do embarrassing things) had slipped her little hands inside of one of the sleek openings between the buttons of Mr. Thomas' shirt, and was twirling his chest hair around with her little fingers. My husband and I quickly began chiding, "Cierra! No! Stop! Don't do that! Keep your hands to yourself!" As we scolded her, that poor man attempted to put her down, but she wouldn't let go—of his chest hair. It was as if someone was paying her to hold on for dear life to the strands of that man's chest hair and to laugh about it. The more we pleaded, the more she laughed. I'm convinced that during embarrassing moments there is an evil force that slows time down and causes us to live through those horrifying moments in slow motion. That is precisely what happened that day. My daughter had a handful of Mr. Thomas' chest hair and it took us what felt like one hundred hours to get her to finally stop. Mr. Thomas gratefully put her down and forgave us as we apologized repeatedly for what had just happened.

Number three: Finding yourself in disastrous situations will be commonplace.

The winter of 2013-2014 was no joke. As a friend of mine so eloquently put it: "It's like Old Man Winter was on Viagra." There were several days that we couldn't leave the house because government officials ordered everyone to remain inside, unless it was an emergency. I can't tell you how many times I felt that my situation was life or death, and because of that I would be completely justified in recklessly driving down the street. I rationalized that if for nothing else than to preserve the ounce of sanity that I had left, as well as the lives of my children, who I repeatedly threatened to throw out in the snow. One Saturday evening after receiving yet another warning from the weather man that a blizzard was coming, my husband suggested that he go to the store to stock up on food, since it was evident that we'd be stuck inside again for at least a few days. The snow had started and it was beginning to look like snowmageddon outside, but I felt the need to leave the house one last time before it got too bad to leave. My husband felt the same way, so we loaded up the circus and headed to the supermarket. The closer we got to the store, the more it snowed. By the time we got there, it was snowing like crazy so against my better judgment, I agreed to remain in our van, while my husband went inside to get the groceries. Picture it: Me and the circus in the van waiting on my husband. The wind was blowing; it was snowing like crazy, and freezing outside. For some ungodly reason my husband parked near the back of the parking lot.

I turned on the radio in hopes that the music would keep my children calm. Once again I was wrong. In no time the ten-year-old and the five-year-old were arguing like cats and dogs, while the three-year-old began chanting.

"Stop it!" Cierra shouted.

"But I just want to know what it would be like to pull one of your lungs out!" yelled five-year-old Tre'.

They argued in that manner for what felt like fifteen days, all while the three-year-old repeatedly chanted about goldfish crackers.

I couldn't take it anymore and shouted, "BE QUIET!"

The silence lasted for about thirty seconds and then everything started again.

Their combined shrieks were enough to make me contemplate fleeing into the snowy night, but I chose to threaten them instead. "You are going to be quiet right now, or you're all going to get it! I mean it! SILENCE! NOW!"

They knew I meant business, and my threat had worked. There was silence until Joshua shrieked, "Help! I have to go potty! BAD!"

I swear a lump formed in my throat. This couldn't be happening. There was no way I was hauling the circus into the cold and into the store. That's when I discovered my saving grace—an empty Burger King cup in the cup holder. I quickly got Joshua out of his car seat, pulled his pants down and told him to pee in the cup.

He exhaled loudly as he relieved himself.

"Ewwww!" Cierra and Tre' yelled in unison.

"Be quiet! He had to go, okay?" I snapped.

And that's when I heard a stream spilling onto the floor. There was a hole in the cup.

Number four: Sometimes you will laugh at the misfortune of your children and that's totally OKAY.

Cierra was nine at the time and had been inquiring about me arching my eyebrows.

"Can I watch you do that?"

"How old do I have to be before you let me arch mine?"

I've told her that she didn't need to worry about any of that right now. Why didn't I know that she'd actually try it? I mean seriously, my kids try everything. I should've known better, but this one caught me off guard.

The next morning Cierra slowly strolled into the kitchen with her head down. When she looked up I noticed a portion of her left eyebrow looking extremely black. Far blacker than the rest of her eyebrow, and even more blacker than the hair on her head. To be exact, that portion of her eyebrow was blacker than midnight.

"Um, Cierra? What happened to your eyebrow?" I asked.

"Um, I…um…mommy, it's bad."

"Yeah, I can see that," I said. "Now go to the bathroom and wash that stuff off."

Cierra returned with a portion of her eyebrow missing. All I could do was stare at her as she tried to explain.

"Mommy, I was trying to arch my eyebrows, but it didn't go the way I wanted it to."

I was afraid to ask, but somehow I knew I had to. "What did you use?" I asked.

"Mommy, please! I was up all through the night praying for a miracle!"

"What did you use?" I repeated.

"Mommy, I kept praying and crying but God didn't answer my prayer! My eyebrow didn't grow AT ALL during the night!"

"What. Did. You. Use?" I repeated louder.

Cierra's eyes welled up with tears as she hung her head and mumbled, "Toenail clippers."

I wanted to scold her. I wanted to tell her that that was unacceptable. But all I could do at that moment was laugh until tears streamed down my face. That's right. I laughed at my child, and it was great.

Number five: Your children will insult you often, without even knowing it.

So my stomach isn't nearly as flat as it used to be before I had children (refer to the last sentence of the second paragraph in number one). My five-year-old loves to cuddle and specifically loves my stomach. The other day he hugged me and said, "Mommy, I love your tummy so much. It's feels like ten thousand marshmallows."

Number six: Your children will hear you having conversations with other adults and may attempt to use some of the words they heard you saying. This usually provides great comic relief.

When I was expecting our third child, I often conversed with a friend who was also expecting. I didn't realize that my daughter was listening to my conversations until one day when Tre' hurt himself. I could hear him crying in the other room, so I shouted: "Cierra what happened to Tre?"

She replied, "I think he tore his placenta!"

Number seven: You will be amazed by the amount of love your heart can hold for your children.

So, I refer to my children as a circus, and at least once a day I have a moment where I want to tear all of my hair out and hide, but I love those three kids more than I ever knew possible. They light up my life, and I couldn't be prouder to be their mom.

Motherhood is a gift from God and I thank Him every day that He chose to bestow this incredible gift on me.

Gina Johnson is an Executive Marketing Assistant at Brown Girls Publishing. She was published in the original Motherhood Diaries and has recently completed her much anticipated debut novel, The Eleventh Hour. To keep up with the happenings of her and her "circus" you can "like" her Johnson Family Circus page on Facebook. She resides in Southwest Michigan with her husband of thirteen years and their three children.

Diary of a Mortified Mom

By Regina Cooper

As a child, I always wondered what my parents did after my brother and I went to bed. At six years old, I was the oldest, and I would try to stay up late every night by asking questions, helping my mother clean the house, folding laundry, or anything else I could think of that would allow me to stay up just a few more minutes.

My mother always caught on to what I was trying to do, and I always ended up in the bed adjacent to my brother's, at exactly 8:30 pm, mad that I couldn't stay up later than Reggie Jr., who is two years younger than I.

One night, I decided not to play any games and I went straight to bed when my dad told me it was time. Going to bed didn't bother me on this particular evening because I had a plan. I was going to lie in bed awake, and when I was sure that my parents were partying without me, I was going to get out of bed and join in, hopefully unnoticed. I didn't bother to include my brother. He was scary, and besides, he would be asleep long before the festivities jumped off.

I was totally unprepared for what I saw when I crept out of bed that night.

My parents, having gotten too careless in their "playtime," were having sex on the living room floor. I guess they never thought their obedient children would ever wake and sleepily wander in, becoming horrified at the sight.

I went back to my room and promptly threw up all over the floor by my bed. Then, I climbed in and went to sleep. I never could "unsee" that. Even today, at 36-years-old, I am haunted by the memory. I should have stayed in bed. And I should have remembered that adventurous couples should wait to be adventurous when their kids aren't home.

Fast-forward 23 years.

My husband, at the time, was always asking for sex. He didn't care if I was tired, at times telling me to just lie there and make an "O" with my mouth, and he would do all of the work! (This is part of the reason he's an ex-husband now).

One Saturday afternoon, after showering, my husband began his Keith Sweat-like begging for "just a taste." I acquiesced, and allowed him a "taste." I closed the bedroom door, making sure to lock it, just in case our young son woke from his nap before we finished. I must admit, I was enjoying myself, oblivious to anything other than the warm sensations coursing through my body. My husband could put it down!

When we were done, my husband appropriately fell asleep (I could put a little sumthin' sumthin' on him, too!) and I emerged from our bedroom happy and satisfied. Our son was sitting on his bedroom floor, watching TV and playing with his Matchbox cars. He looked at me and smiled, and I smiled back and asked him if he wanted a snack. He nodded, and I went off to grab him a box of animal crackers.

About a week later, I was driving home after picking up my son from preschool, and a song came on the radio. I immediately changed the station, as it was inappropriate for a four-year-old to hear. Without delay, my son asked me to change the station back, because he liked that song. I told him no, and further explained that I didn't think the song was suitable for his young ears.

"Why not?" he asked again.

"Because that song is about sex, and I don't want you walking around singing about 'Birthday Sex'."

"Why not?" He wasn't giving up. I had to think fast.

"Because, you don't know what sex is, and mommy isn't ready to tell you right now. I will tell you all about it when you're older, and you will understand better then." I know, not the best explanation, but it was all I could come up with at the time. *Hindsight is 20/20.*

"I know what sex is!" he blurted out. And my heart skipped a beat. I began to sweat and my cheeks got hot.

"What? Who told you?" I asked nervously.

"Nobody told me. I just know," he said confidently.

"Okay, then you tell me, what is sex?"

"It's when you eat each other's winkies," he said, and smiled proudly.

I could have died right then and there. Except I was driving and could not even see an opportunity to pull over and catch my breath. Swerving into the left lane and back again, I tried to remain calm.

"Ummm…uh, what? WHO TOLD YOU THAT?" I tried to keep my composure, but my blood pressure was rising.

"I told you mommy, nobody told me. I saw daddy eating your winkie, and you were making nice noises."

I cried. Then, I laughed. Then, I tried to convince him that he saw no such thing!

"Ha ha ha! Oh baby, Daddy wasn't eating anything! He was... he was... he was checking mommy to make sure that she was clean down there. I had just gotten out of the shower, and I asked Daddy to make sure I washed good! You know, kind of like when I check to make sure you wash behind your ears! You know?" I knew I was failing, but there was no way I could have my baby boy thinking that sex was "eating each other's winkies" and "making nice noises." At least not yet. Not now. He was only four years old! *And didn't I lock that damn door?*

"Ooooookaaay Mommy," he seemingly finally gave in, "but I SAW Daddy eating your winkie!"

Again, I did everything I could to convince him he was mistaken, and he finally began to doubt his own eyes and agreed that because he had just awoken from a nap, that maybe he thought he saw something he really didn't.

I felt relieved. Well, relieved at least until he's old enough to know what oral sex is. Then, he'll think back to the day his Mommy picked him up from preschool and lied to him about Daddy "eating her winkie."

Oh, well, he's ten years old now. I figure I've got at least, what? Five more years before he asks me about it again? Right?

Right?

Regina is a 36-year-old mother of two boys, ages two and eleven. She's been married to her husband Steven, for four years and teaches sixth grade Language Arts and English as a Second Language. She has appeared in several plays and a few movies, which filmed locally in Houston. She loves to write, act, sing, listen to poetry, and of course, teach!

Diary of a Grey-haired Mother

By Edna Pittman

Let me start out by saying I'm not old. I'm actually only in my thirties, but you'd never know it by my hair.

I always knew I wanted three children, so it was never a surprise to me when that's exactly what I ended up with.

When I had my first child, I was excited for everyone to see her. In my eyes, Deja was the prettiest baby ever born. That was 1997 and I couldn't wait until she was six weeks old so I could take her out of the house. My mother and grandmother forbade me to take her out before then, and I'm not even sure why. I guess they thought she would get germs.

So, at six weeks I rushed down to the local photo studio to get her first pictures taken. She had the cutest pink and purple outfit with a cute pink bow in her hair. The photographer was nice and kept telling me how gorgeous she was as she snapped shot after shot. Back then, you didn't get to proof pictures before you purchased them. I waited three weeks for those pictures. The day they called, I rushed to the studio to see how beautiful they were. I opened the huge package as the photographer watched. I pulled out an 11x13 photo of my precious baby. I couldn't believe my eyes; everything was in place but one finger. Her middle finger stuck out as if to say... well, we all know what that means.

I immediately pulled out the rest of the pictures hoping they all didn't look like this! I started to cry. I was devastated. How could I give people a picture with my child flipping them off! Only nine weeks into motherhood I realized I was not in control. That was also the first time I noticed a single grey strand of hair on the top of my head.

Destini is my middle child. Everything about my pregnancy and her birth was easy! She was an easy baby. This little girl had the sweetest disposition. For the most part, she was completely happy, healthy and very smart. She once drew a picture of people with little chickens all over their bodies and told me they had the chickenpox. How cute is that? She made friends everywhere she went. She would sing a solo for anyone who asked and she never seemed scared to do it. The only time I ever saw her upset was the day after her baby brother was born. When she came into the hospital room, it showed on her face. We were all excited, but she didn't want anything to do with him. She didn't even want to look at him. She was always so sweet, so it really shocked me. When Demarion came home from the hospital, it didn't get any better. She did not understand why this little boy was around, taking up everyone's attention. She wanted him back in my belly.

When her brother was only a month old, she'd obviously had enough. One day, I heard a scream and my baby started crying. I ran to see what was going on and Deja told me Destini had thrown a book at him! I was livid. I didn't understand how this sweet child could do such a thing. She was the good child. She wasn't setting trashcans on fire like her older sister had once done. She taught me that even my sweetest child could do something not so pleasing, but I would love her just the same. After tending to the scratch that was left under my son's little eye, I noticed a patch of grey hairs creeping through the dark brown hair that filled my head.

Demarion is my third and last child. He's my only boy. Having two girls before him didn't prepare me for a thing. There were days that I was convinced my son invented the name "terrible twos." The girls were calm at two, not this child.

I can thank him for every single grey hair on my head. Who would imagine this cute little child could be a holy terror? My mother always said her grandchildren were good, Godly children, but Demarion might have been the exception.

It all started the moment he took his first step. Nothing was safe from his wrath after that. He terrorized his sisters. They couldn't have friends over without him chasing them with a sword or throwing size D batteries at them, hitting them in the head. He terrorized me also. I will never forget the day he came to me with a huge smile on his face and insisted that I come see what he had done. He was just learning to talk so his "Mommy, come here" sounded more like "Mommy, some ere." I don't know if I remember it so well because I was cooking, or because what I discovered scarred me for life.

As I walked into the room he shared with Destini, I noticed something all over the wall on his side of the room. He jumped on his bed with the biggest smile and pointed to what he obviously thought was a hand-painted masterpiece. My first thought was, *Look at this mess; he's going to have to clean this off of my wall!*

So, I said "That's nice, honey!"

As I got a little closer, I noticed that his side of the room had an awful smell! So, I asked him (because he was being potty trained) if he had pooped in his pants. The look on his face said it all. As I reached to grab him from the bed, I realized his hand was covered in poop!

Totally disgusted, I freaked out. I'm sure I had an out-of- body experience because I had never been so angry. That lovely masterpiece on my wall was definitely a Demarion Pittman one-of-a kind, made with his own poop! I didn't know what to do other than scream at the top of my lungs. My husband came running in the room and immediately realized what his pride and joy had done. While he was disgusted, he thought it was funny how angry I was. I grabbed Demarion and whisked him into the shower. All I remember is me yelling, "*That is so nasty!*" and him looking at me with the cutest puppy dog eyes. He had no idea why I was literally scrubbing him with a towel while he stood in the shower being hosed down like a three-alarm fire.

In my mind, I had obviously failed *this* child because my girls never did such a thing! Where did I go wrong? What would make him think this was okay? It didn't take me long to realize that Demarion would challenge and defy everything I thought I knew about motherhood.

There were always trips to the emergency room. I was convinced that Child Protective Services would come knocking on my door because this child was always hurt. On this particular day, as I rushed into the ER with him in tow, I prayed that they wouldn't think I had done anything to him. I guess my hysterical state let them know that, once again, Demarion had done something crazy. I felt like these people were beginning to know me, and I was right.

As I rushed to the counter with him on my hip, the receptionist smiled and said "Hi you guys!"

I began to explain why we were there once again. I have no idea why Demarion was so rough and stubborn. At two years old, he fought other kids at daycare, beat up and harassed his sisters and challenged my authority in every way.

Today was no different. It all started with a simple request, "Put the pencil down." Those four words had me standing in the ER. I was passing through our living room when I noticed Demarion sticking a pencil in his ear. I tried to reason with him and explain that he shouldn't stick pencils in his ear because it could hurt, or someone could accidentally hit his hand and the pencil could burst his eardrum. Obviously, he didn't understand or didn't care because after my second request, he just jammed it in his own ear! I was mortified! Blood immediately began to squirt from his ear. I was so afraid that I began screaming for the girls. They put on their shoes and we were off to the ER again. My daughters kept asking why he would do something so crazy and I just didn't have an answer.

Now, we were sitting in the hospital room waiting for a doctor to come in. The entire time I just prayed that first, nothing would be wrong with his ear and second, I wouldn't be contacted by CPS.

Luckily, the doctor was extremely nice. He assured me this kind of thing happens all the time with boys this age. He checked his ear, cleaned him up, and tested his hearing only because I insisted. Thank God nothing was wrong with his ear and we could go home with no worries. I'm quite sure the grey hair count went up significantly that day.

This boy definitely made raising girls look like a cakewalk. There was never a dull moment with him. He ate dirt and wrestled our dog to the ground, all while his daddy proudly smiled and declared "That's my boy!" I was at a loss. I began to notice grey hairs sprouting out all over my head. The girls did funny things, sometimes embarrassing, but funny.

Deja had a fascination with breasts when she was four. One day when I picked her up from school, her teacher pulled me to the side and asked if she could show something to me. She pulled out Deja's artwork, and I immediately noticed that all of the women were wearing bras. While I was a little embarrassed, I thought it was funny. That was simply her way of showing the difference between girls and boys.

Demarion, on the other hand, constantly did things that could actually cause major damage. His sister, Deja, has horrible allergies, so I've always had to keep medication in the house for her. One day, she needed the medicine. It was grape-flavored and all three of my children had taken it before. I gave Deja a dose and sent her on her way. Demarion wanted some also, but I explained he didn't need any. There was no fussing or crying. He seemed to understand and it was no big deal.

Several minutes later, Destini tells me Demarion is drinking the medication. I ran into the kitchen to find the empty medicine bottle on the floor. I had no idea how he had gotten it because I had put the cap on the medicine and placed the bottle in the highest cabinet. Well, that didn't stop him. He opened the lower cabinets and climbed onto the countertop, where he stood tall enough to reach that grape yummy stuff! I smelled his breath and it was evident he had drank the medicine. I thought I was going to have a stroke. I had just taken him to the ER a month ago for his ear. How could I possibly show up there again with this child? I was angry, but scared to death. What could a whole bottle of this stuff do to him? I immediately called the poison control hotline because I didn't know if I should just call 911 and have him rushed to the hospital. I explained what happened and the woman calmly asked how much he drank and his weight. I said, "The whole bottle. It was new!"

She explained that he would soon begin to act extremely hyper and to keep a close eye on him. She told me not to let him fall asleep anytime soon. For two hours, it took me *and* my girls to watch Demarion. This boy began running into walls full-force, knocking himself to the floor. He was yelling and screaming like a madman! It was almost impossible to stop him. We eventually had to try to hold him down. His heart was beating so fast that I thought he was going to have a heart attack. After two hours of constant running, screaming and destroying our nerves, he stood in the living room, looked at me and passed out on the floor. I thought he was dead! I realized he was breathing, so I called the hospital and talked to a nurse. She told me it was normal after an episode like this. He crashed hard and although I was worn out, I stayed up for hours watching him while he slept. I kept praying he was fine. Needless to say, he woke up the next morning back at it, like nothing had ever happened.

As a mother of three, there have been times that I thought I was going to have a heart attack, pull my hair out, or lock myself in a closet. I've spent many hours praying that they wouldn't make me lose my mind, and that they would grow up to be exactly what God called them to be.

As they all get older, I realize that I can laugh about almost everything they've put me through. I've thought about dying my hair and have even made my oldest pluck a few of the greys because they seem to be taking over, but I now appreciate that every grey hair on my head has a story.

I'm sure the bulk of my grey hairs arrived the day another unfortunate incident changed Demarion's life forever. I'm just happy I can still remember all of the crazy things he did before he was even three years old. I've convinced myself that I have many more years of memories to make, so I might as well embrace those silver strands.

Not one of my children is the same and that's what makes them so wonderful. Each of them brings something unique to my life and I wouldn't trade it for all of the money or dye in the world. I get three times the fun, followed by three times the exhaustion. One thing I know is that my life is ridiculously better with Deja, Destini and Demarion in it, so bring on the grey.

Edna Pittman resides in Oklahoma City, OK with her husband and their three children. After a devastating accident left her caring for a special needs child, she worked with legislators in Oklahoma to get Demarion's Law passed. She is a Television Director and Founder/CEO of the non-profit organization BARI (Being A Real Influence). Find out more at www.Demarionslaw.com.

Diary of Justabusymom

By Andrea Odom Campbell

One of the struggles I always encounter with my kids is dividing up the chores. As formerly sheltered kids who weren't really required to do much around the house, life with the now divorced "single" me as their mommy has certainly taken on a different view. I tried to explain to them that no one works for them and that we all have to contribute to keep this household afloat.

My boys were honored with the task of folding and taking everyone's clothes to their room. Yep, it was laundry day! In an effort to further the mythical illusion of teamwork (yeah, right), I piled all of the clean laundry on the couch and told them to work together until it was all finished. This is not too much to ask from kids who are nine and ten, pretty realistic expectations, right? Who was I kidding?

As soon as I left my room, the oldest son came to tell me his younger brother was not helping. So, I begrudgingly left my desk to go see what the problem was. Looking around,

I saw a basket on the floor, which contained maybe thirty percent of the clothes and the remaining seventy percent were still in occupy-couch mode.

My middle child's philosophy was clear; he would do the laundry in the basket and his older brother would fold what was on the couch. Fair enough? Oh, I don't think so kid.

As I attempted to calmly explain to him that's not an equal distribution of labor, he got mad and started to throw a fit nine-year-old middle kids style. Go figure.

Now I have very low tolerance for this kind of stuff, particularly as I try and encourage my kids to talk about what's bothering them. I am not from the school of thought where folks just blow up and fly off the handle. Blame it on my psychology degree, but I believe in just talking it out, expressing yourself calmly….words make things much easier, right? This clearly wasn't the route he chose on this given day. And in my all-or-nothing parenting style, I said "Fine! Guess what? Since you want to fall out and lose it, here ya go. You now have the privilege of doing it all by yourself! Now go straight to your room!"

A fit, a few foot shuffles and some tears later, he retreated to his room with me dragging the basket behind. My instructions were very clear. Do not leave this room until all the clothes are folded. He plopped on his bed miserably, as if the entire world just came crashing down on his sweet little shoulders.

Don't you love how when one kid is in trouble, suddenly the "free" kids are now super sugary sweet and quickly capitalize on the punishment of their fellow man? Sad order of events, I know. Both my youngest and oldest were being over-the-top helpful, you know, how the non-grounded kids like to swoop in and garner all the positive love and attention available?

As I moved on about the evening, helping with homework and getting dinner started and as time passed, I wondered how much progress he was making. I passed by once, put my ear against his room door just to make sure that he had turned on the TV and all was silent. Figured I better take a look and see. When I opened the door, to my surprise, this little boy was curled up, fast asleep on top of the pile of laundry. I had to laugh, matter-of-fact, I should've taken a picture and posted on Instagram! Hashtag #lazy! I woke him up and insisted he get busy and he finally got moving.

The evening was full of regular duties, making dinner, reading books, and a little TV time. All peppered with appearances from him here and there, dropping off piles in everyone's room. He seemed happy, decently productive and for all practical purposes, going with the flow. The crying had subsided and the attitude seemed to shift back to normal. All was well in his world!

After the other two went to sleep, he came in my room and asked if he could read to me. *Aww so sweet!* Of course, I said yes. I tucked him in, told him I love him, and we talked about the lessons learned from the experience of the evening. I told him I was so proud of him for finally finishing and kissed him good night.

The next morning started just like any other day. I got up early to get dressed before the kids rose for school. As I made breakfast and got everyone moving, my oldest came in and said he didn't have any socks. Looking perplexed, I walked to the Laundry King's room to inquire. I asked where were his brother's socks. Denying any culpability, he shrugged his shoulders and moved on to brush his teeth.

I looked in my daughter's room. No wayward socks. I looked in my drawers. Nothing. As I continued my inquisition, I could see him begin to squirm uncomfortably. *Deny deny deny. Come on kid, fess up where did they go? Did the laundry fairy take it?* I smelled a cover up.

I decided I would leave him in his room, close the door and let him figure out how he was going to work his way out of this one. I know my child. I know his thought process and knew if given time in solitary and a short rope, he would hang himself!

Upon my return, he had pulled a suitcase from the closet and therein, was ALL of the missing laundry! I was furious on the outside but dying LAUGHING inside. He really had just put it all in a bag and sent it packing! I've got to give him credit, though, because I am hip to the hide-everything-in-my-closet-when-I-don't-want-to-clean-up trick. Naturally, the closet was the first place I looked, but I never in a million years would have pulled out the suitcase!

My poor baby. He lost his phone and television privileges and shed some more tears for getting busted in the biggest laundry smuggling ring to ever hit our neighborhood. With every tear and every hard time, my hope is there's always a lesson (and some damn funny stories) on the other side.

I see their growth. I see the progress and I know the next time he will do it with a little less attitude and maybe will have clean socks and underwear, too.

Andrea Odom Campbell is a mother of three ridiculously busy children, a philanthropist, social media enthusiast, smart ass, taxicab driver, juggler of schedules and believer of all that is good and righteous in this world. With a tongue-in-cheek comedic angle, she addresses the realistic sexy and not so sexy sides of being a mom. Follow her as she chronicles her shortcomings as a parent, struggles with discipline, cooking, co-parenting post divorce with "the artist formerly known as husband" and anything else she sees fit to throw out her not so expert opinion on. Visit her at www.justabusymom.com

Diary of a Big-Hearted Mom

By Latrice Martin

Dear Diary,

I have been known to have big hair, big thighs, a big smile, and most importantly, big dreams. But apparently there was one thing about me that is big that I had no idea of and I never expected a child to tell me about it.

My husband and I usually agree on most things about parenting. We mainly agree to let me lead the way with the child nurturing and he can handle the discipline for the most part. When the kids are out of control, I get to yell, "I'm going to tell your daddy!" They panic and act correctly. My own daughter has said that she doesn't cry when I discipline her. When the kids are hurt or need assurance, daddy sends them to me so that I can love and hug on them. It works. We settled whether to tell them about Santa Claus and the Easter Bunny during premarital counseling. I said to leave Christmas and Easter to Jesus and he reluctantly agreed. What we didn't discuss in premarital counseling was what we would call the children's body parts. I said a penis is a penis. He said they should call it a "wee wee." I said a vagina is a vagina. He asked me, "Well, what is the other name you use for it?"

I replied, "Vagina." I was not going to let my daughter walk around using terms like "coochie." I can't even write the other words. Now there are plenty of other nicknames that one could use for these body parts. A penis could be called a dick, pee pee, or wee wee, I suppose. I always thought that it would be harder to determine what was wrong with a child if they went to describe their body parts by nicknames. My husband thought there would be some shame in them using the correct terms. His reasoning made absolutely no sense to me. It could be because I am one who thinks that I know everything. It's not at all because I am a teacher, either. So, from the moment that the children were born, I have used the correct terminology for all body parts. I told Davin he had a penis, Taylen she had a vagina, and Madden that he had a penis.

My two youngest are just sixteen months apart so I raised them like twins for the most part. Although Taylen is a girl and Madden is a boy, they took baths together for the first two to three years of their life. It was just easier that way and I have no shame in it.

It was actually during bathtime when Taylen realized that she didn't have what Madden had. She told me that her vagina "was broke." I was baffled and I asked her what was wrong. I thought she was getting a urinary tract infection and there was possible pain. She told me that it was broken off because it did not look like Madden's. Now I had to explain to her that all boys had penises and all girls had vaginas. Her vagina didn't look anything like her brother's penis and it was not broken. It took some time but they soon realized that Daddy was also a boy and so he also had a penis and mommy was a girl so she had a vagina. The discussions never had to go further and I was very satisfied with that.

Whew!

One crazy evening, my kids were running around the house like they usually do. I was screaming for them to stop running and threatening to tell their daddy. My husband would hear me and then use his daddy voice to get them to stop. I sat on the couch resting and relieved that they had finally calmed down a bit. Then, just as quickly as they could, they all flew down the stairs and burst into my bedroom. We hadn't taught them about knocking on doors yet and so I didn't stop them. The most they would do is catch their daddy playing his video games. Well, from there I heard another door get pushed open. I can now hear my husband tell them to get out of the bathroom. But they didn't. All three children stopped dead in their tracks. Madden shouted out, " Oh, Daddy has a penis!"

Davin, being the oldest said, " Yes, Madden we all have a penis because we are boys."

Madden replied, " Oh well, my penis is not big like that."

Taylen chimed in and said, " Well, I am a girl and I have a vagina and it doesn't look like that!"

My husband was horrified that they didn't leave, but even worse, he was listening to his baby girl talk about her vagina. He told her to leave immediately and talk to me about her vagina. I don't know why because I didn't want to hear about it either.

Taylen ran into the living room to recap the whole conversation. She told me that daddy had a penis and so did her brothers. She said that Madden said his penis wasn't big like daddy's. I agreed. She told me that her daddy made her leave the bathroom. I explained why. Then she said she had a vagina. I told her that she was correct. She told me that I had a vagina. I told her that she was correct and that I do have a vagina. Then she said, " I am a little girl and I have a little vagina!" Then she stretched her arms out as wide as a four-year-old could and she proudly said, " But you are a grown-up and you have BIIIIIIIIIIIIIIIIIIIIIIIIIIIIIIIIIIIIIIIIII IIG vagina."

I just sat there on the couch. I didn't know how to respond to her. Didn't know if I could tell her that vaginas stretch but I believe that they go back to their regular size. I didn't know if I needed to explain to her that I had C-sections so no baby had ever even come out of there to stretch my vagina. Finally, I didn't know if I should tell her that having a big vagina is not a compliment, but actually something that no woman would want to have. So I just sat there on the couch and looked at her. She gave me a hug and ran back upstairs.

I have had big accomplishments, big disappointments, big surprises, big goals, big vehicles, big closets, and I do love having my big hair. But I never knew I had a big vagina. Why didn't she say that I had a biiiiiiiiiiiiiiiiiiiiiiiiiiiiiiiiiiiiiiii iiiiiiiiiiiiiiiiiiiiiiiiiiiiiiiiiiiiiiiig heart?

Latrice Martin is an Elementary School Teacher. She is married and has three children. She lives in Houston, TX. You can follow her on Instagram @trice421

Diary of an Overwhelmed Mom

By Stephanie Bullock Ferguson

"Hey, Foxy. You sure are lookin' good."

Over forty years ago, that pick-up line wasn't considered corny. Well, it wasn't as corny as it is today. It was, however, effective and that was all my dad needed. That little phrase was the beginning of a life my cool-as-summer-breeze-dad and my initially-totally-uninterested-at-the-time-mom couldn't have scripted any differently.

The tall, lanky returning Vietnam Veteran set his sights on the Curvy Girl who lived down the road from his sister. He made it a point to walk by her parents' house every single day. She may have been playing hard to get, but she knew who he was, he was sure of it. Much to his dismay, he was wrong. She didn't know him at all. All she knew was some "fresh" soldier was giving her a hard time while she was trying to get groceries at the local market.

"Do you mind if I come see you some time?" he pressed.

With as much attitude as one could have while sporting a head full of hair rollers and cut off shorts, she shot him a quick look and an even quicker answer, "Sure." She then headed out with her signature strut.

The next day, the Vietnam Vet showed up at her parents' house. But he and the Curvy Girl were both in for a surprise as two other suitors showed up, too, all within minutes of each other. Shocked that they all had the nerve to just pop up on Christmas Day without being invited, the young lady let them all know where they stood when she got in her car and left them there to entertain themselves.

Thankfully, the grocery store crooner wasn't easily deterred. After a lengthy pursuit and a traditional courtship, a horrible car accident proved the Vietnam Vet was the real deal and Mr. Otis Bullock and Ms. Leedrester Hayes were married on June 13, 1970.

Their union proved to be as eventful as their first meeting. Like every other couple, they dreamed of starting a family and living happily ever after. Also like every other couple, they didn't anticipate just how difficult starting a family and having a happily ever after would become. Seven years into their marriage and they were still childless. Time after time they were heartbroken, and finally decided to consider other options. Even in the 70's, the idea of adoption was still a very private, almost taboo subject. Yet, regardless of popular opinion, they knew they had the love and the means to give a child the kind of home all children deserve.

Finally, the day came when they were to meet with the social worker to begin the process. The usual polite chit-chat dominated the beginning of the conversation. Soon, they were hitting the meat and potatoes of the reason for the interview. When asked if they wanted a boy or a girl, my parents' answer was as full of personality as they were. It was such a passionate answer, it actually turned into an argument right in front of the social worker. The social worker that they were meeting for the first time ever. The social worker who was going to determine if they could be trusted to raise a child. Still, they couldn't come to an agreement and left the much-anticipated appointment feeling like unfit parents. Their dream of little feet running around their home wasn't any closer to reality, or so they thought.

Fortunately, the social worker was good at her job and was able to see their true dispositions. She saw their passion was easily translated into love. The adoption process continued and the young couple was hopeful once again.

Soon, the big day came when they were to pick up their new baby. They made the almost two-hour drive to the capital in what seemed like only a few minutes. The love they already had for the baby that wasn't even theirs yet was already overflowing. Boy, girl, no longer mattered. At this point, it was about loving their baby with everything they had.

The couple anxiously entered the dark, drab office building and began to wonder if this closed adoption was actually a black market adoption. Once again, the astute social worker reassured the couple they were in the right place and also on the right side of the law.

Then, the lady who had gotten to know them pretty well dropped the news they never saw coming. On March 3, 1977, they had been approved to be adoptive parents. On March 5, 1977 a set of fraternal twins was born. A boy and a girl. They had been placed for adoption soon after their birth. The social worker couldn't think of a more fitting couple for a boy AND a girl sibling set than the couple who had left a lasting impression after that first meeting. After seven long years filled with both physical and emotional pain, the Vietnam Vet and the Curvy Girl down the road were still not going home with a baby. They were going home with two.

The Brat Pack, Double Trouble, The Terrible Two, Twin Power, The Reign of Pain. However you chose to label the stork's two-for-one deal, the parental training wheels come off a lot quicker when the first child is twins.

Today, my mother is the family matriarch, proudly loving nine grandkids. Mama is now a Four Star General of Motherhood, but in March of 1979, the General was only a Private. When my brother and I had just turned the corner into the famed season of the terrible twos, we took on Private Mommy in a surprise attack. After a grueling defeat, her only recourse was to document the battle details so an accurate historic record would exist. Plus, she needed to be able to remind my father of the day he broke the code and left a man behind when he left her home alone with toddler twins.

There was no journal available on the battlefield. The era of laptops, tablets, and smartphones was still decades away. Even digital cameras were an unknown. The worn and overwhelmed novice was forced to use the tools of the ancients, plain ole paper and ink. Though she was speechless, the sword of her pen was able to capture the happenings of the "Twin Campaign" like only a mother could...

Before 6:45am, on Saturday morning, March 24, 1979, Stephanie did the following minor jobs:

1. *took my brand new tube of lipstick and wrote on her new shirt and pants, the wall, Stephen's bike, the carpet, and even saved a wee bit for her face and mouth; oh, forgot about the bedspread too.*
2. *pulled the ends off a box of Q-tips*
3. *tore my hair rollers into three pieces each, and*
4. *pulled the shade down from the window.*

After she woke me to tell me she wanted to eat some grits, just when I thought I could sleep at least until 7:00am, I discovered the damage. While trying to salvage some small part of my bedroom (all of the damage was in my room), I guess she felt she had better make a quick getaway. She climbed five shelves to the top of the bookcase to get her bank down, dropped it, and broke it in at least 100 pieces.

Now Stephen has gotten up. They have joined forces against their mother. Lights are going on and off at the force of four little hands, all their daddy's shoes have been removed from his closet and neatly thrown around the house, toys are all over the house (the toy box is empty), and now Stephanie is spraying Stephen with Fantastik cleaner. I guess he looks dirty to her.

It's 7:00am now. I should be just starting my day, but I have lived three days in the last 15 minutes. They have just begun. I wonder what is in store for me next. I'm afraid to look!

Please, please, won't someone rescue me?

The record of the events for that March day has stood the test of time. Soon after, Private Mommy had the entry laminated then sealed it with The Mommy Curse: "I hope you have one just like you." She placed it in our baby book as a reminder for herself and a warning for others not to be fooled by the cuteness.

Thirty-five years later, the General now remembers the battle with a wise grin, satisfied that the curse not only worked, but it kicked some serious booty.

Currently, I have a four-year-old who never— under any circumstances— sleeps past 6:30 am on any given day.

My almost three-year-old tears whatever he can into little teeny, tiny pieces, and my six-month-old makes sure I'm up until at least midnight, then wakes up around four every morning. She remains awake just long enough for me to have to get out of bed and make it to her room. Then, she quickly goes back to sleep as if the sound of her crying on the monitor was just my exhausted imagination.

It is safe to say that I will probably never sleep in on a Saturday ever again. My brother, Stephen, now has six kids ranging from age eleven to age two. No need to elaborate on how the curse repeatedly slaps him in the face. Either way, curse or no curse, General Mommy will never forget the Siege of 1979.

Stephanie Bullock Ferguson is the mother of three small children, ages four, three, and six months. She has been married to Lamar Ferguson for over eleven years. She is a native of Southern Mississippi and currently resides in Austell, GA. She can be reached at smbullock_99@yahoo.com.

Diary of an Uninformed Mother

By Keria Burkhalter

I married James Burkhalter Jr., who I lovingly call June, in July of 2005. We were supposed to spend five years of marital bliss together before we started to have kids. But God's plans were not ours. My birthday is at the end of September and I wanted to have a few alcoholic beverages that night, but my cycle still hadn't started. So, on my birthday, when I got off of work, I stopped at the store to buy a pregnancy test. I couldn't believe what I saw on that stick. I was just trying to be responsible but I didn't really think I was going to be pregnant.

When I told the love of my life the news, he fell down on the bed in shock. I know that seems a little dramatic, but he didn't think he was ready to be a father. I did not want to be a mommy that soon either, but that all changed.

In May, not even a year into our marriage, James III was born two weeks earlier than scheduled but he was perfectly healthy. In the months before he arrived, I researched everything related to babies, so I would be able to make educated decisions. I spoke to other mothers, especially my own mom, so I could be as prepared as possible. I decided to nurse him since it's healthier for the baby. Neither my mother, nor my research told me that I would start so soon though. I nursed him for the first time just hours after he was born, but he had no problem latching on. James was like his greedy mom. He was not going to pass up food.

What my research also failed to inform me of was the pain associated with feeding my baby with a body part. My mom didn't even tell me that I would experience the worst pain ever because of breastfeeding. I know my baby was hungry but did he have to chow down, literally? I remember pulling him off of me while his jaws were still clamped down. OUCH!

When his teeth started coming in, I made the easy decision of weaning him. I couldn't handle that pain anymore. The money I spent on formula was worth the savings in my upper body parts, well the little bit I had left. It just felt like he chewed them off. But things weren't always painful. We had wonderful moments.

I returned to work the day after my six-week medical leave ended. I wasn't running away from my child. I just loved going to work to get a break. I didn't know I would be so tired. My mom didn't tell me about that. The exhaustion, however, would disappear when I saw James III smile or when he started cooing. I would pick up my child from the babysitter and go straight home.

Once we got settled, I'd whip out my phone and start taking pictures of the next new thing he did. My phone was loaded. I enjoyed showing off my cutie. I know everyone thinks their kid is cute, but mine really is. I didn't think I could ever have enough photos of my baby. My husband said you could watch James III grow up on the camera, kind of like the process of a cartoon. I may have gone overboard a little but I didn't want to miss a minute.

As he grew, I noticed how intelligent my little boy was. Every mother thinks their kid is smart, too, but mine really is. He would wait until I left his room to remove his diaper and wipe the boo boo on the wall. It was really smart not to do that in my presence. Yes, he was punished for that (after he made a second attempt). My mom didn't warn me about these moments.

He also had great timing. James would wait until I was about to leave the house to make new smells in his diaper. I couldn't arrive at my destination with a stinky child, could I? So I had to stop everything to change his diaper and sometimes his clothes when he decided to have a blowout. That's when the contents of the diaper can't be contained. Mom didn't let me know about that either.

There was so much she and my research failed to warn me about. I didn't know I would get super powers once I had a kid, did you? I could leap bounds to reach James, who was about to touch something dangerous. I could also rush to the sound of the crash with Superman speed to find my son near the dresser that he decided to pull open all of the drawers to climb up the top. I thank God he lived through that so he could start the real fun, school.

I loved his first day of preschool. He was so excited and I liked his teacher. James was growing up. When he started kindergarten, I loved his teacher. She was from another country and spoke English differently, but she got the point across. She didn't yell in her class. She would lower her voice so that the students would have to quiet down to hear her. I thought it was genius.

By that time, I was raising my voice at home, so I wanted to know if it would be effective for me. It wasn't. She must have had more special powers than I did.

One day, the school's number scrolled across my phone screen. My mom didn't tell me how to remain calm when that happened. My heart pounded louder and faster than ever. I answered the phone with fright oozing from my pores. Once his teacher confirmed that nothing terrible had happened she informed me that James was being disruptive. He was perfect in preschool, so I don't understand what happened, in Kindergarten. This is when we first started noticing "the payback."

Now, that is something I remember my mom warning me about when I was a little girl. She would tell me that my children would be just like me and I would get all of "this" back. I didn't know what she meant. I know now, though. James was a talker like me. He wouldn't keep that mouth shut long enough for his ears to activate. (Remember, I told you he was super smart). Every report card that he brought home had an E (Excellent) in all areas that he studied. But the comments nearly contradicted the grades. His teacher would reiterate how great of a student he was but always reminded us of how much he talked in class. It's like James went back in time and looked at my report cards. This was payback at its finest. Since I'm still a talker, I don't know how to fix it. I've tried all kinds of punishment. He does well for a while, then he goes back to the same habit. We're still making adjustments with James III.

Well, apparently we weren't having enough fun with just one kid. I started getting the itch when James turned four. So we tried and tried. Finally, we got pregnant. I wanted a girl so bad I could taste it. Just days before I found out what I was going to have, a friend of mine lost a child during her pregnancy. That put things into perspective for me. I no longer cared what the gender of my baby was. When my doctor told me that I was going to have another little boy, I was happy that he was still growing in my womb. We decided to name him Jace. June and I also discussed how we thought Jace would act. We just knew that he would be quiet. He was at first, but I'll get to that part.

On March 6th, while in my eighth month of pregnancy, I was put on bedrest. March 8th, at my scheduled check-up, my OB-GYN told me to walk over to the attached hospital to get monitored. I had pre-eclampsia and my blood pressure was higher than my last checkup and I had some contractions. Once I was admitted, my doctor wouldn't let me leave. They induced my labor, on the morning of March 9th and at 3:15

pm, Jace entered the world. The delivery was just as painful as my first. So, I thought everything was normal. My parents returned to Denver, Colorado and my sister to Wichita, Kansas.

However, on March 10th, the pediatrician on call told me that Jace had a loud heart murmur. We left the hospital on March 12th. My dad returned to Tulsa just in time to help his son-in-law take his family home and help June clean up the house that was ill-prepared for the new addition. He also journeyed with us to the first visit with the cardiologist on March 13th. This was just one week after I was put on bed rest. I know that's a lot to take in, but imagine how we felt. When we met with Jace's cardiologist, we had a lot of questions and concerns. However, she helped ease some of that. She remained calm as she explained that they would monitor him. Jace's condition persisted, though, and when he was just four months old, my baby had heart surgery. It all happened so fast and could've been one of the most stressful times in my life. But when a big event happens, I'm able to leave it in God's hands because I can't control it. I mentally prepared for whatever the outcome would be. Good or Bad. Jace had a ventricular septal defect, which the head pediatric surgeon completely corrected. Jace also had pulmonary stenosis. The surgeon did the best he could to repair it during the same surgery.

June and I had lots of family (in and out of town) for support and I was grateful for everyone that returned so quickly. Jace pulled through. However, what I wasn't grateful for was the "hidden" work the surgeons must have performed while they had my son opened up all that time.

I think someone turned up the volume in his voice box while in surgery. Jace screamed louder than ever when he came home. Once we figured it wasn't from pain, I couldn't believe what I was hearing. We thought that his little body was working so hard to keep his heart beating that the lungs were forced to take a backseat.

My once very quiet little child was turning into a pro-screamer. This boy hollered just because he thought it was a great thing to do. I finally learned his screams and figured out that he wanted to eat. I felt like a cow. I was prepared this time, though. I greased my "teats" with cream that prepped them for the grueling pain. I really tried to nurse him longer than his brother, James, because I thought Jace could benefit more since he had the heart issues. But he was a biter, too, so I only nursed him two months longer than his brother. That was not the only difference between James and Jace.

The boys got along very well. James was almost six years old when I gave birth, so he was extremely helpful in the house, as long as the television wasn't on. If it was on, then I had to use my "outside" voice to get his attention. (I told you we're making adjustments).

Jace came out looking just like me, but when I look at all of the old pictures of James, he looks like his brother, too. I think that's the only similarity between the two because they act nothing alike. It amazes me how children can have the same genes but be completely opposite.

James is my loving child. Jace is my fighter. (I guess he needed to be). We had to wait until Jace was ten months old to get him circumcised. Additionally, not even a month after his first birthday, Jace had to have a heart catheterization to repair the pulmonary stenosis that the surgeon couldn't completely repair during the first surgery. But now Jace is doing well. He pulled through it all and I'm grateful. But again, I'm not as grateful for what happened after those hospital visits. My mom didn't tell me it was going to be like this. Jace's strength increased after his procedure. That is a bad combination for a kid that likes to hit. You would think he just watched old boxing movies all day with his technique. He had us all fooled.

The boys were playing like normal and Jace hit James. It must have hurt because James started crying. Jace tiptoed to him and quietly asked, "Do doh daaaa?" which, in Jace-ology means, 'You okay?'

That's sweet, right? Wrong.

James looked up and started laughing, acting as if he was never hurt. So Jace started punching him. His one-two combination was serious. His hands were quick. By the time we started reaching to stop him, he calmly stopped and walked away to play somewhere else. Don't worry. James wasn't hurt badly. That just made us start watching Jace a little closer. He might be dangerous when he gets older. *Do they have boxing for one year olds?* We're looking for ways to channel that energy.

June is a drummer and is trying to help Jace with his hands. He plays the drums on anything that will make noise, like his daddy did when he was a toddler. Now June and Jace spend time honing that skill. When he's not drumming, Jace uses his quick hands to perform other tricks, like pulling off his diaper to examine the contents. I can't believe I forgot that. I re-learned that I can't leave him alone for very long either. *Are you thinking what I'm thinking?* My mom did not warn me about that either.

I want you to know more than I do, so let me warn you about a few possibilities. Things can be perfectly fine one minute and then, poof, a complete mess can appear, like lotion all over.

Your child can also disappear from you in a store. That was a scary feeling so I have the boys on a tight leash, not literally, well, not yet. Your child can scream at the top of his lungs in a restaurant over and over and someone can make a nasty comment about it, to which you must reply, "I know my kid is loud, but could you suggest what you did to silence your children?"

Your kid can find a marker and write on his white door, after you've cleaned it up many times before. In our house, I can't always tell which kid did what because things become blurry after the second child. My mom didn't tell me...wait... she may have told me...I probably wasn't listening. Kids!

Keria Burkhalter is married and is the mother of two silly boys. She lives in Tulsa, OK and can be found on Facebook. She can be reached at mrskeria@hotmail.com.

Diary of a Map Maker's Daughter

By Nikki Woods

Sometimes you work and plan and save up for the perfect family vacation, and then sometimes, you just look up and it's happening.

December is the month of miracles. It just is. Don't get me wrong, I can point to unexplained grace and favor lifting us up in big and small ways all the time, but maybe we're just more open to receiving during the month we celebrate the ultimate miracle.

Part of my job as the senior producer for a nationally syndicated radio show is to coordinate guests that appear on-air each morning, including the entire gamut of African-American movers and shaker from T.I. to Tyler Perry... Snoop Dog to Oprah... the Queen of Hip Hop to the President of the United States.

That puts me on a first name basis with the people who handle their business and in the case of President Barack Obama, the director of African American media for the White House is the man to know.

After years of going through all the behind-the-scenes stress and strategies involved in linking up the leader of the free world to our eight million listeners, it was a wonderful feeling when the White House via Kevin, sent my family an invitation to tour 1600 Pennsylvania Ave.—the official residence of the First Family.

Most people may not realize what goes in to getting the President on the air. It begins with either our wanting to book him for certain segment or their request to come on the show and the ball usually starts rolling one week in advance with a call to or from me or our show's Director of Talented Services to, or from Kevin S. Lewis. From there, times and dates are coordinated as well as the talking points or what will be discussed. The President always sounds casual and laid back on the radio but it can be high pressure for the team of people working behind the scenes for him and us.

I can't tell you how it feels to hear the words, "Stand by, the next voice you hear will be the President of the United States."

Especially when it's a President that I had known as a state Senator and then voted for in the history-making election.

I was present for his election night victory celebration at Grant Park in Chicago —the city where I lived and worked for ten years. It was a surreal evening that my co-workers and I were blessed to be part of. The energy was indescribable... every media outlet and personality you could imagine was there, along with major celebrities, politicians and Civil Rights icons. We considered it an honor to be there to perhaps witness history, but for him to win? Wow! I still get chills as I remember what it was like to see the President-elect, Michelle, Sasha and Malia enter the stage as the First Family. I thought it about what it took for them to get where they stood… as well as what it took for me to be standing where I was. Like most African Americans, I thought of my parents and how they couldn't even imagine a night like this would be possible in their lifetime. I thought of my generation, who was so full of hope and as Election Day got closer and closer and wondering could this *really* be happening. I thought about how many times I'd told my sons they could be what ever they wanted to be and now, I could finally believe it wholeheartedly.

Whew! It was a lot to process *and* do my job at the same time.

I wished everyone I knew and loved could have been there to feel what we felt.

Then, in January of 2009, we were in Washington DC chronicling history once again, braving the massive crowds and freezing cold at the President's first inauguration.

It's funny how our lives are mapped out long before we know where our journey will lead us.

Who knew when I landed at Howard University, a naïve teen with hopes of becoming a journalist, that years later, I'd be back in "the District" to play a role in broadcasting the first official speech of the 44th President.

I took my co-work to my old stomping grounds for some good ol' Jamaican cuisine, conjuring up memories, good and bad about my college life.

I almost wished I could return as an undercover student just to tell the young women that almost none of the things that seem important now will matter twenty years down the road. Not the boys, the clothes, the clubs or the cliques. But of course, who would believe me? I'd sound like a parent, and what college student wants advice from mom and dad? I sure didn't. In fact, if I was majoring in journalism, I was minoring in escaping from my parents.

But dad had another plan. In fact, because his job as a mapmaker for the United States Government called for frequent travel, sometimes, with no notice, he would pop up on campus. Making "Your dad is looking for you," the six most dreaded words I wanted to hear as a student spreading my wings for the first time.

Born in Kirkwood, Mississippi, my daddy and my hero (grew up without a mother), put himself through college, graduate school and law school, married my mom and raised two daughters.

Oh, and at one time, he was also was a four-term mayor of Rock Hill, Missouri, the St. Louis suburb where my sister and I were raised.

Dad lived his life with just the kind of purpose and precision you would expect of a mapmaker: orderly, deliberate, and to the point.

He knew what he wanted in life and went after it. Thankfully, he chose the kind of woman who supported him and his dreams and he'll be the first tell you that my mom... his wife, business partner and helpmate is still the love of his life. His children, my sister and me, were a close second. And he knew what he wanted for us as well.

One mission was for us all to visit all 50 states... by station wagon, and later, a van. Dad would take as many family members as his vehicles could hold. Some summers included cousins, others grandparents and aunts, pre-seat belt years when kids could sleep untethered in the cargo area along with the luggage.

Eventually, we did make it to every state, visiting landmarks and relatives: the kinds of things that only mean something later on when you can hardly remember the details.

Years later, we still take family vacations together— all orchestrated by Daddy. Eventually, grandchildren and sons-in-law were included. Young men were taken by the way my dad lived his life and loved and provided for us and our children, too. He became a friend and mentor to many who probably wondered how he makes it look so easy.

Most of my adult life I've tried to find ways to give back a portion of what he's given to us.

TV journalist Bryant Gumbel laments that his greatest regret is that his beloved father never witnessed his success. Not a moment of it. His dad, Judge Richard Gumbel died suddenly in 1972. One week after Judge Gumbel's funeral, Bryant's career started to boom.

At some point, I realized I'd never be able be exceed what my parents have done for me, or even break even.

What I could do, though, is include them as much as possible in our lives without imposing on time they have set aside together enjoying their retirement.

The line from the movie "Mahogany," may be corny and overused but that doesn't mean it isn't true. Success really *is* nothing without someone you love to share it with.

And let's be clear. Success is relative. It doesn't necessarily mean rising to the top of your profession or having tons of money. Success is any goal you set out to accomplish and are victorious... from kicking an addiction to raising a happy healthy family.

Including my parents in this trip was more than a chance to spend time with them, it was more a chance to witness them and my boys do it together—three generations visiting the White House.

So, we loaded up the truck and headed for D.C.

Well, sort of. What I did do, is deal with Dallas's December "arctic blast," (can't we just call them ice storms any more?), purchase plane tickets, schedule back surgery (don't ask), and all the other things I do day-to-day with two sons, ages eleven and twelve. Oh, did I mention we'd just moved into a new house?

But we made it happen and were thrilled that mom and dad could join us. Even though you can never repay your parents for all the sacrifices they've made for you... inviting them to the White House is a good start.

My boys got an interactive history lesson no classroom instruction can match. They learned when the White House was built, how it's run, how many rooms there are and the significance of being there while the sitting president is the first African American to be elected to that position.

There are some other things I hope they will come to realize, too:

1. We live in an amazing country in an amazing time where we have the freedom to play "Candy Crush" while we wait for our turn to tour the White House.
2. We should cherish every moment with our family—some day everything will become a distant memory.
3. Sharing your blessings is a gift for the giver and receiver. I can't imagine what it would feel like to gain the world and its riches and not have my family. Watching this great moment through my children' and parent's eyes was priceless.
4. The difference between a house and home. We visited the part of the White House meant for the public. But on another floor that we weren't privy to is where the President and Mrs. Obama have built a home for Sasha, Malia, and the First Lady's mother, Mrs. Robinson. Always reserve time and space for your family that includes a peaceful place for you and

those you love to unwind, recharge, eat, praise, be yourselves, keep traditions and start new ones.

5. My Daddy is the Man. No disrespect to the President but to watch my father walk into the Oval Office (when he really wasn't supposed to) reminded me of how much things have changed and how much they've remained the same. My dad—strong, black, intelligent, articulate, stands tall and feels worthy enough to walk into any open door.

A line in Rudyard Kipling's classic poem goes:

> *If you can talk with crowds and keep your virtue, or walk with Kings—nor lose the common touch...if you can fill the unforgiving minute With sixty seconds' worth of distance run, Yours is the Earth and everything that's in it, And—which is more—you'll be a Man, my son!*

I don't even want to imagine all the hurt, the disparities, and obstacles my dad must have had to overcome as a sixteen-year-old black man with roots in Mississippi. My mom, born and raised in Jamaica, came to the United States alone as very young woman to attend nursing school. These two are beneficiaries of the best America has to offer. They are truly testaments of how pride, dignity and a long faith journey can pay off in later years.

I've had several weeks since our trip to put these words on paper. But at the time, when I watched Daddy saunter into the President's office, like any grown child who sometimes switches roles with their parents, I beckoned him, teeth clenched and possibly a hand on my hip, "Daddy! Get out of there! This isn't your office!"

The twinkle in his eye told me. "It *could* be."

I hope my sons will be just as confident.

They have the greatest role models in the world, President Barak Obama… and my dad.

Nikki Woods is a Multi-media personality, Social Media and Personal Branding Coach, Motivational Speaker and Voice-over artist, and the CEO of Nikki Woods Media. She is also the senior producer of the acclaimed, nationally syndicated Tom Joyner Morning Show (TJMS), the most successful syndicated urban radio show in history reaching more than 8 million people on a daily basis. Her "Mamas Gone Wild" website and weekly blog entries on BlackAmericaWeb.com highlight—with insight and hilarity—the ups and downs of being a hard-working radio producer by morning, an ever-patient classroom mom by afternoon and adventurous mother of two by night. As a highly sought after keynote speaker, who serves as both an OWN ambassador for Pretty Brown Girl Inc., Nikki has earned the title of Global Visibility Expert and continues to reach millions and growing using multi-media to empower and train audiences with messages and methods for excelling in business, marketing and personal growth. Find her on the web: www.nikkiwoodsmedia.com.

Diary of an Autism Mom

By Janoah White

OMG... if this child of mine "elbows" one more random stranger or little baby, I'm clicking my heels three times and telling Calgon to take me away... because that's probably about as far as I'll actually escape.

There's never a dull moment with my teenager. When he was diagnosed with autism at age two, if you had told me all the random things we'd go through, I would never have believed it. If you'd told me that when my son became a teenager, I'd still be in the exact same mommy mode as I was when he was a toddler, all the way down to not being able to go out because I didn't have a babysitter, I would have told you to hand me ALL the wine. Immediately. Please and thank you.

But the whole elbows thing? He got it from school a few months ago. It's very cute and basic, but it needs boundaries. I can't explain to him enough that some people don't know what it means when he walks up to them, announcing "elbows," while simultaneously offering his elbow in hopes of receiving an "elbow bump" in return.

Furthermore, not everyone is receptive when a five ft-eleven-inch tall, black male child approaches them, invading their personal space, shouting "elbows" (or anything else) with his elbow in their (or their kids') faces.

In his innocence, he doesn't understand why he can't approach everyone. He doesn't get that he might scare or intimidate some people, especially little kids. He means well, so he expects it to be received well by everyone. And in a perfect world, it would be. But the world's not perfect. And in this season, in his mind, elbows have taken over.

Dang! What happened to hello? High fives? Handshakes? Daps? Fist bumps? You can get all that with my son. After elbows. Can't we save this for our friends and the people we know?

All day long. Elbows. Elbows. Elbows. Pretty girl? Oh, she's definitely getting elbows. Old lady? You get elbows, too. Salesgirls in the mall get them all the time. I guess he figures if they approach us, they HAVE to pay him attention. And they always do.

Guys get the cool, laid back elbows, less often than the females, of course. I get elbows all day long. I don't mind them, though. Like I said, I think it's cute. SOMETIMES.

I went to his school for a program one day, and got to meet the classmate he always speaks of who also does "elbows." I don't know who got it from whom, but I found it so funny that my son made sure that this other child came and gave me elbows. Like five times. It was hilarious and he was super excited that his classmate and I were able to share that moment.

It's not as cute when he runs off and offers his elbow to random unsuspecting strangers. Thankfully, some people are good sports about it. Little do they know that their small acts of kindness are a huge deal to me. I'm surprised they can't hear the sighs of relief in my soul when they're nice to him. I almost want to run up right behind him and give them hugs. Hugs, hugs and more hugs. (Who's doing the MOST now?)

I'm always grateful for those who accept my baby... I mean my big boy... exactly as he is. Those who don't judge him, don't look at him funny, don't seem annoyed. Those who graciously accept his greetings by smiling and giving him the elbow, which makes him happy. And when he's happy, I'm happy. He's trying to be social and friendly, and I want him to be. I want him to find positive ways of interacting with others. I have to keep reminding myself that.

I guess there's a sense of apprehension on my end because everyone isn't so friendly. I don't want his attempts at friendliness to be taken the wrong way, by the wrong person. Some people simply don't understand developmental challenges. It makes them uncomfortable. I've learned that I can't expect everyone to understand. I just have to appreciate the ones who make an effort.

I always wonder if I'm too high-strung for not wanting him to approach strangers. Am I stifling his social skills? Am I making him feel wrong because his impulsivity isn't the norm? Should I just let him be? Really, I'm just concerned about his safety, so why do I feel so confused about it?

I should get over it and be glad he's no longer walking up to random people touching or taking their iPhones... as often as he used to. Now, at least he only does it to certain people that he knows. That phase, where he was sure that everybody's technology belonged to him, seemed to last FOREVER. If anybody had an iAnything around us, I had to be quicker than lightning to keep him from trying to get it. Thank God that's calmed down! People will fight over their phones. Shoot, I'll fight over MY phone. I never want us to be on the negative end of a misunderstanding.

I still remember how I felt when he was first diagnosed. Terrified. I had no idea what the future would hold for us. Nor did I know how to deal. I didn't know if he would be able to communicate, or to what degree. I didn't know how to parent a child with special needs. I was young in my early 20's. He was my firstborn I was *just* learning how to be a mom. Then I had to learn to be so much more. The journey has, at times, been overwhelming and draining, but also a lot more rewarding than I ever would have imagined.

We've learned so much, and we've both come such a long way. There are many things I'm still figuring out as we go along. Like puberty. I need ALL the prayers to deal with *that* on some days.

But he's so smart, loving and full of personality. I couldn't have asked for a better match in a son. He's perfect for me. Who would have thought that because of my son's social skills (not social deficits) and magnetic character, I'd develop relationships with so many people that, otherwise, I never would have?

I thought "I" was the friendly one. He might have me beat, though, when he's in the mood to be bothered. Come to think of it, I guess he really *is* my mini me. He ignores people when he isn't in the mood. (I just isolate myself, so I don't come off as being rude.) But we can both be social butterflies when we feel like it. The difference is, I wait for opportunities— he creates or forces them.

His personality is so interesting to me, because he's withdrawn and indifferent one minute, but borderline assertive the next. He's gonna deal with you when he's ready to. Or when you have something he wants. And you're GOING to pay attention! But don't bother him when he's not in the mood because you'll probably be ignored. If not for autism, I might be offended. I'm sensitive!

Even though I know not to be offended, sometimes that whole ignoring me thing? Not good.

I remember a time we were in the grocery store checking out. He saw one of the machines that sells the instant lottery scratch off tickets (another obsession), and asked if we could buy one. I told him no. He knows not to walk off from me in public. Often, I hold his hand so that he doesn't, as he's always been one to dart off.

As I'm paying for the food, he knows I'm distracted (oh, he's very smart and calculating), so he ignores everything I said about no ticket and no walking off, and runs and pushes a button on the lotto machine for a $5 ticket. Guess he figured that was going to be his only chance. Problem was, the guy who was ahead of us in line had just put money in the machine and was in the process of buying his own tickets. *Whoops!*

He turned around in disbelief and I couldn't apologize and explain autism fast enough. My fear was real. Where I come from, you don't mess with people's money. The guy was cool about it, though, once I explained. I literally thanked God as I saw his immediate anger melt to fear, and he told my son that he'd probably chosen a winning ticket. Forgiving and encouraging. My relief was immeasurable.

I think all "autism moms" deal with safety concerns and social concerns. We're always on our toes. Any parent has to expect the unexpected, but when you have to literally anticipate someone's every move in order to keep them safe, it can become overwhelming.

Even though Shawn's a teenager now, I have to still provide the same attentiveness I did when he was little. I'm like stalker mom. Eyes in the back of my head. Hands and feet as quick as lightning. He's calmed down some over the years, but he's still an impulsive ball of energy. And he's content being him. We get the side-eye from people sometimes, and we also get stares. It is what it is, though. I try not to let it bother me. It doesn't bother him in the least, so I mentally tell those people to kick rocks and keep it moving.

Everything isn't quite so tense. We have a lot more low key moments as well that I can't help but laugh at when it's all said and done.

Like the morning I realized my toothbrush had been bothered. I called him in the bathroom and ask if he'd used my toothbrush.

"Yes," he said.

"Why?"

"I was racing."

"What do you mean?"

"I was racing the toothbrushes," he said, matter-of-factly.

"I don't understand. What do you mean racing the toothbrushes?"

"Racing the spinbrush pro (his) vs. the Sonicare." (i.e. my generic spinbrush— not a Sonicare).

Oh...so our toothbrushes are having competitions now? What could I say besides, "Don't ever touch my toothbrush again, and never use anyone's toothbrush except your own"? And a quick prayer to God that he's never "raced" my toothbrush before.

I was annoyed at first; I'd just bought my lil' generic toothbrush! (Don't judge me!) But I also laughed. How does he come up with this stuff? The experts say kids with autism don't participate in pretend play? Duh!!! This one does.

By the way, his toothbrush won. (I had to ask!)

I'm just glad my son is who he is, quirks and all. I do wonder what's next, though? What's going to be the new "thing" my adult-sized, kid-at-heart is gonna fixate on, especially as it relates to others? He really likes people, so I just want it to be something that doesn't scare anyone off. Is it going to be invasive of their personal space? Is it going to be more low key? Is it going to make me miss elbows?

Well, I kinda feel like elbows will last forever. I guess only time will tell.

Janoah White is a fulltime mom, former radio producer and freelance writer living in Chicago, IL. She holds a Master of Arts degree in Journalism and a Bachelor of Arts degree in Television, both from Columbia College Chicago. She shares random thoughts via her blog at dontjanonogood.blogspot.com, and on twitter @ dontjanonogood.

Diary of a Mom Who Shoots From the Hip

By Deborah Gaffney

I am always intrigued by the notion that opposites attract; probably because my husband and I can be described as polar opposites. He is incredibly logical. In fact, I'll nickname him Dr. Spock because I love Star Trek. Dr. Spock believes that everything has to be planned, have a purpose and be carried out accordingly. I, on the other hand, find most elements of structure mundane. Yes, I totally understand the purpose and reasoning for structure; but really people? Sometimes you just need to relax and shoot from the hip.

I have an "A" type personality so I want to be in control and I'm somewhat ADD. Okay, I admit I am a lot ADD. If I sit still for too long, my body's reaction is to go to sleep. Since my type "A" personality wants to be in control, falling asleep when idle for too long is not cool. When I'm sitting, I somehow remain in constant motion. Having children allowed me to mask my inability to sit still because I could hold them, play with them, rock them, sway them and shoot from the hip. I got out of a lot of otherwise-boring scenarios because I needed to refocus my children's attention to thwart them from the dreaded temper tantrums that I had heard and read about.

Let's be honest, there are some moments when we, as adults, want to throw a tantrum because some event, activity or business meeting is such a waste of time that you end up screaming inside your head. Children haven't learned to control those impulses yet, so tantrums happen.

So imagine my Vulcanly logical husband shaking his head in utter confusion when the children would excitedly tell him about their adventure of the day over family dinner. Imagine him looking at me and asking "Why would you go park hopping when there is a perfectly good park in the neighborhood? Deborah, you shoot from the hip."

Now, I will admit, the first time he used that phrase, I was mildly insulted. I have since toughened up. Every time I did something that he considered unplanned, he would say, "There you go, shooting from the hip." Finally, I learned how to holster my guns and say, "Bang, bang! I'm shooting from the hip. We may go to the beach today or the library, or just stay at home."

There are many ways in which to hop. Ladies, some of us are very good at shop- hopping. The beauty of the hopping strategy is that the ADD personality does not get bored, or fall asleep, and children love being on a constant adventure.

Bang, bang.

On any particular summer morning, after breakfast and a tantrum possibility meter check, we would gather up the necessities and load up the then-popular minivan. Yes, we did later graduate to the Texas-sized Suburban. Trip hopping necessities included a potty chair for anyone not yet potty trained and anyone who needed an emergency potty break. Water, fruit, a change of clothes or three, and a general plan for adventure. It is extremely important to at least know the first closest park so the children can get out and run. We would play on the swings, slides and other equipment. Running games included hot lava, tag, freeze tag, Ring around the Rosie, London Bridge... after thirty minutes or so, they would be ready to enjoy a car ride with their favorite sing-along songs to the next adventure. I believe their favorite activity was stopping to pick up food and picnic during a park hop.

Outdoor games at various parks, pools, zoos and museums are fun. There is an inherent danger when games like hot lava are brought into the house. Hot lava is when the children declare the floor is hot lava and if you step or fall on the floor, you die. Imagine, if you will a room full of furniture. I mean, come on, you can't play it unless you have something to climb onto, otherwise the lava will get you. Since I am writing this story, we, all survived.

Bang, bang.

Well, one evening I could hear my son yell from upstairs, "Hot lava!" And the sounds of jumping and running played on my kitchen ceiling as I prepared a dinner that I shot from the hip. I am not a gourmet cook, there is a lot of attention to detail in that task. My caffeine uptake would have to be significant to allow for extended dinner preparations. So I'm listening to my favorite radio station, playing my favorite music, and I hear a very loud CRACK from the ceiling. I run upstairs to see what's wrong and my three darling children are sitting demurely, watching television. *You know where I'm going?*

I asked them what was that noise, and they replied, "What noise?"

So, to ferret out the hidden event, I ask them what they are watching on television. Of course, they don't know when thirty seconds ago, they were playing hot lava. But I sit down, on my beautiful leather couch to "watch television" with my three angels. When my body arrives at the cushion of the couch, there is no support and I virtually sink to the bottom. The children, my angels, look at me and I look at them. I feel the anger rising as I think of the repair bill for this sofa. I rise and walk to the back of my sofa, lift it up (as we have on so many occasions when we are playing "cave") only to find the 6"x 9"x12' piece of SOLID wood has been cracked in two.

Well, bang bang!

Then, of course, the culprit was offered up in an attempt to save the group from punishment. Remember the object of hot lava is to not touch the floor, because it's lava and you will die. My angels, were jumping from love seat to ottoman to couch and the oldest child, jumped onto the center of my beautiful leather couch and the wood, touched the lava and died.

Later that evening, Dr. Spock asked me when I was going to get the couch repaired. I responded, when they leave home. They haven't left yet and the couch is still floating on the lava.

Bang, bang!

Deborah is a wife and mother of three children. She resides in League City, TX with her husband of 25 years. Her favorite comment when asked how she feels about growing older is that she didn't get the memo. She is currently pursuing a career as an Author and Actress.

Diary of a Mother Raising Three Sons (The Joke's On Me)

By Patricia Woodside

"Mommy, I thought only Jesus could bring people back from the dead. How come Elisha did it, too? Did he copy off of Jesus?"

Dear Diary:

It never ceases to amaze me that as many times as I've read various portions of the Bible, my eleven and eight-year-old boys will come up with some observation that never occurred to me, as they did after I read this passage of 2 Kings to them.

I've always heard that God has a sense of humor. Truly He must, especially in that heavenly birthing center when He assigns children to their parents.

As the mother of three sons, it can be difficult to keep up with the testosterone that flows as freely as tap water in our home. Every day brings a new challenge, whether it's nursing the one who ran head-on into a doorjamb; dissuading the one determined to leap like Spiderman off the staircase; getting picked last for a rousing game of touch football because I can neither throw nor catch that pointy, semi-round ball; or navigating the terrain without gouging my feet on one of the myriad of LEGOs infesting our residence.

At five-foot-two, I'm height-challenged— a decided disadvantage in our family. My husband is nearly six-foot-seven, yes, more than a foot taller than I, which means when the growth spurts finally cease, there will be four men towering over me like oak trees. My eleven-year-old is staring me in the eye and my almost nine-year-old is already past the point of looking up my nose. Another couple of months and they'll be bending over to hug me—or pat me on the head—like their oldest brother, the eighteen-year-old, has been doing for years.

All this would be great if they shaded me from the sun or protected me from the elements, but those things would require them to surround me without stepping on my toes, walking over me or otherwise knocking me to the ground because their feet are longer than a twelve-inch ruler.

Eighteen, eleven and nine—even their ages are another of God's jokes. For the longest time, I thought I'd be the mother of one. Not one of my boys was easy to conceive, although all have been a blessing. The oldest came after surgery to remove nine fibroids, followed six uneventful months later by a trip to Paris to get away from the whole conception thing. Who knew the little one we sought would hop on board the family's train, so to speak, somewhere in between Hubby and I walking the streets of Paris and all those rich, late night French meals?

He would prove to be a blessing in many ways. Our only daughter came a short two years later after more infertility treatments. Sadly, she didn't survive her birth. Spina bifida coupled with hydrocephalus snuffed her out before she got started. All my hopes for someone to share the girly things with, like sparkly fingernail polish, romance novels and marathon trips to the hair salon, died with her. I do get to share some of the things my mother taught me with my boys. They love my baking—from cakes and cookies to chocolate éclairs and cinnamon rolls, they expect multiple goodies per week—but they pretty much aren't feeling any of my other attempts to share—no sewing, no keeping a diary and no home perms. We buried her, and I descended into a walking despair.

But I had a little one, not quite two years old, and he didn't know anything about death. All he knew was sliding down his Fischer-Price slide in the middle of our living room atop my $1,000 rug in footed pajamas, eating oatmeal for breakfast every single day, hanging out with his grandparents at the church-run daycare, and dissolving into peals of laughter when the slightest thing tickled his funny bone. He wasn't my salvation, but he saved me. He made me do when I had no do left in me. My despair came out in other ways—weight gain, hair loss, melancholy moods—but that little boy never ceased to put a smile on my face.

After losing my heart, the years passed, and passed…and passed. Then, with more infertility treatments, we conceived Middle Son. I was so afraid. Would I lose this child too? That pregnancy was the roughest of them all. I was scared but thrilled when he decided to enter the world two months early. Allergic to everything but air, feeding him brought new challenges. He weighed the least of all my children and ate almost nothing, yet he looked like a baby sumo wrestler.

Having two sons was nice, good even. We'd pretty much decided to close up shop, but God wasn't done chuckling. Not 30 days after we began a new chapter in our family's story by relocating from New York to Florida—with most everything we owned still in boxes lining the walls of our new apartment or in a storage unit—Baby Boy let his presence be known. A finger stuck blindly in the Yellow Pages got me to a doctor who confirmed the good news. Maybe this last one would wear a skirt, I thought, but no. What did God give me? More testosterone and urine around the toilet seat.

I have to laugh, though. What isn't funny about giving birth at 42, threatening my OB/GYN in my best mafia voice that if she doesn't thoroughly tie/cut/burn/shred everything related to having babies, I'll hunt her down and feed her to the fishes? Who doesn't like frequent trips to the supermarket's hair color aisle just so none of the Baby Boy's classmates mistake his mom for Grandma? What mother isn't excited when she realizes she may get to celebrate her youngest child's high school graduation and her retirement with one party?

These sorts of things make me laugh. Honestly, the thing I love most about our boys is that they keep me laughing. It's said that laughter is the best medicine, right? That's a good thing because I'm going to need a lot of Ben-Gay, rubbing alcohol, ibuprofen, and maybe even some prescription meds by the time I'm done raising them.

My favorite thing is simply spending time with our boys. Any activity, whether hanging in the kitchen, at a sporting event, watching TV, at church or simply reading at bedtime, leads to fun and laughter. All of my boys are readers, I'm proud to say, just like their mom. Of course, our taste in reading material varies greatly, me being partial to romance, women's fiction, historical novels, biographies and the occasional non-fiction/self-help book. Oldest One, an athlete/budding musician, likes sports biographies and fiction featuring young Black men like himself. (Like they have a lot of *those* in bookstores!) Middle Son, the future astronaut, likes fantasy. He can't get enough of Harry Potter, Rick Riordan's Greek mythology-based tales, and talking, warring sharks. Then there's Baby Boy, the artist, who also likes fantasy, but is just as enamored with comics and graphic novels.

The one book we all enjoy is the Bible. If you never thought reading the Bible was an opportunity for side-splitting laughter, you might want to dust yours off and dig in again. In our home, some of the strangest questions and most interesting discussions come during bedtime Bible reading. Some questions are expected: *How come everybody in the Bible was so old? What's wrong with Pharaoh that he needed so many plagues to get it? Why do the Israelites keep making God mad at them?*

Then there are the questions that follow some of the most cherished, kid-friendly stories in the Bible. When I was young, we heard the stories, learned the stories, and accepted the stories. At least that's my recollection. Today, I'm not sure whether kids are smarter or if PlayStation has impacted their brains, standardized tests and food preservatives.

Take the story of Noah. Rather than focus on God saving the animals and the people who were righteous so He could restart civilization, the boys pepper me with questions like "Where did they put all the animal poop for 40 days?" and "If everybody on the boat was already in Noah's family, then who did they marry to start new families?"

At times, their observations are a bit more abstract in nature, like when Baby Boy asked, "If God is everywhere, does that mean He's watching us when we go to the bathroom? 'Cuz that's nasty."

As a mother, I already wear a multitude of hats—home manager, financial adviser, chef, seamstress, housekeeper, tutor, even chief playmate and BFF. I consider myself fairly well acquainted with the Scriptures, having been in church my entire life and even having served as a pastor's wife for a duration, but now I have to add Bible scholar to my repertoire?

Yes, God definitely has a sense of humor. I imagine that every time one of my boys—or any child—does or says something a little precocious and way too intelligent, something that elicits one of those deer-in-the-headlights, blank stares in response, God chuckles and cracks a knowing smile.

Anticipating Tonight's Crazy Question...

Patricia is the 5' 2", married mother of three sons, all destined to well exceed six feet and to pursue greatness. A native New Yorker, she now lives with her family in central Florida where she works as a business analytics and quality manager. Patricia has published numerous True Romance sweet romantic confessions, two short stories, and several online magazine articles. She owns Story Dazzle Editorial Services and is also an avid reader, book blogger, and aspiring author. However, motherhood is her 24/7 role and the one of which she is most proud.

Diary of a Ninja Mom

By Denise A. Kelley

Summer 2006

Dear Journal,

I've got a good one for you today. I'm going to call it, ***If I have to tell you one more time.***

I had planned a family day trip to the North Carolina Zoo weeks ago. As always, when it was time to go, my husband came up with a last minute excuse as to why he couldn't attend. Of course, I was hot with him, but me being the loving mother that I am I didn't want to disappoint the children, so I refused to cancel.

Wait, now that I look back, he was always bailing on us at the last minute. I think that was his strategy to get rid of us for a day or two. I guess it's true what they say about hindsight, that bad boy got perfect vision.

Anyway, moving on because writing about my babies' daddy is an entry of its own. I called my cousin, Chyra, to see if she was available. That was my road dog. I knew she wouldn't let me take the two-hour trip alone with a five and a six-year-old.

Chyra arrived at my house an hour later and the trip was underway. Tee, my priss-pot of a daughter, who was only six years old at the time, sat quietly in the backseat and enjoyed the sights. On the other hand, my son, Taj, the five-year-old terror, did just the opposite. I presumed when he realized his father wasn't in the car, he temporarily lost his five-year-old mind. He was in that backseat turning it out. Good thing for him I was driving because that hindered me from reaching back and putting my hands on him.

Chyra tried her best to keep him out of trouble. "Stop Taj… Don't do that Taj…No, Taj," she constantly told him.

I told him if he didn't start behaving I was going to call his no-good father. Well, I said the no-good part under my breath, but that threat worked for a few minutes, because Taj did grant us a few moments of peace, but that was short-lived. A few moments passed and then it happened, something was tossed or better yet, thrown up to the front seat. Taj had hurled his little ninja turtle action figure that barely missed my face. The quick loud tapping noise the toy made against the front windshield, along with seeing a blur of something in my peripheral vision made me swerve the SUV. I thanked God out loud there wasn't another vehicle next to us. Maybe he thought he was a ninja child that day, but I was on the brink of showing him that his mother was a Master Ninja (that's even if female Master Ninjas existed). If not, I was getting ready to be the exception to the rule. Prisspot gazed at him with a look beyond her years and rolled her little six-year-old eyes and went back to coloring in her Dora the Explorer coloring book. I caught that in the rearview mirror and chuckled; wondering where she learned that. I guess females are born with the ability and skill to 'roll eyes'.

"I hope they leave you at the zoo," I heard her mumble to him, without even looking up from her coloring book. I know I should have scolded her for that, but at that moment, she was also speaking the sentiments of my heart. He was acting like an animal, so why shouldn't he live with them? Okay, I know that's wrong. Come on now journal, you know I wouldn't really leave my baby at the zoo.

When he realized he wasn't getting the toy back, this child had a meltdown. He was screaming at the top of his lungs while kicking the back of the seat. The fact that he had six more men like it in his Barney the Dinosaur book bag meant absolutely nothing to him. He wanted *that* one. *Jesus take the wheel*, I thought because I was ready to jump in that backseat and hurt my child.

"Why are you being so defiant?" I yelled.

Chyra busted out in laughter. I glared at her because I didn't find anything funny. In between her cackling, like she was watching an episode of *Martin*, she explained it was funny because I'd used such a big word on a child. I didn't want Taj to catch me smiling, so I turned my head and smirked because that was kind of funny when you thought about it, but defiant was the best word to describe his behavior and I wasn't in the mood to come up with a five-year-old word just so he could understand.

We made a pit stop at Hanes Mall in Winston-Salem, NC. Taj was still on his terrorist act kick. I told him to stop running, he didn't listen. I told him to stop touching stuff, he didn't listen. At one point, he told me 'no,' and I almost blacked out on him. I know I threatened him at least ten times. I had to keep reminding myself that he was a five-year-old boy, just to keep myself at bay. I found myself repeating, "If I have to tell you one more time." Those very words gave me pause for thought. If my mother was there at that moment, she probably would have smacked me for even saying that.

When I was growing up, that statement was non-existent in my house. My mother told you to do something one time, and one time only. If she *thought* she had to repeat herself that was going to be your behind. I felt like Macaulay Culkin from the movie *Home Alone*; with my eyes expanded like fifty cent pieces, my mouth wide opened and my hands clutching the both sides of my face. *Ohhh nooo, I've turned into one of those new millennium, time out, go to your room with all your toys, flat screen TV's and devices-type mothers.*

Chyra took Tee to the little girl's department and of course, Taj remained with me. My breaking point finally made its appearance in the shoe department in Macy's. While telling the lady what size I needed in some Steve Madden sandals, Taj slipped away without me realizing it. When the lady strolled to the back to retrieve my size, I looked down and he was gone. I tried to keep calm, but nowadays people are crazy and anyone could have snatched him up; although the way he acted that day, I'm sure they would quickly return him and give me ransom money instead.

I jogged through the store, calling his name. I ran into Chyra and she said she hadn't seen him. Just when I was about to lose it, I spotted him running through the clothes racks. I yelled for him to come to me and that child terrorist kept running in the opposite direction. When I finally caught him, it was on like Donkey Kong. In addition to him acting like he had no home training, I was angry for other reasons. For one, he had me running around the store overexerting myself, and two, he scared me. Now, Journal you know how it is when someone scares you and it turns into a false alarm that does nothing but make you angrier. I grabbed him by the arm and off to the bathroom we went with him kicking and screaming the entire way. I was praying that we didn't pass anyone that was employed with Child Protection Services, because they always seem to pop out of the blue when you're getting ready to discipline your child in public. I didn't care though, if anyone approached me, I was ready to give them an old school answer, *Unless you want me to beat you also, I suggest you mind your own business.*

Taj's wildin' out had driven me over the top. He was acting up in the public, so I was getting ready to act up in public with him. Chyra and Tee followed closely behind us. Taj was crying and reaching for Chyra to save him, but he was beyond being saved at that point. When we made it to the bathroom in the food court, I was sweating from dragging him the whole way. I escorted his little behind in the ladies room and I was glad no one was in there. Chyra and Tee stood outside and the cries could be heard, but not distinguished, beyond the bathroom door.

When Taj and I emerged from the restroom, Chyra lost it again with laughter. I came out all disheveled and you could tell I'd been crying because my eyes were red and puffy. Chyra's only question was *Who got the beating?*

Yes, I was feeling defeated as a mother and questioning what was I doing wrong for him to behave so badly, but rest assured, mama wasn't a Master Ninja for nothing.

Denise A. Kelley lives in Roanoke, VA. Her first novel will be released in September 2014, under the pen name D. A. Kelley. She can be reached at daknovelist@gmail.com, or Facebook: Author D. A. Kelley.

Diary of a Perfectionist Mom

By R. Ellen Crigler

I was born in the perfect month of January, perfect because it starts the year. The path seemed to be perfectly laid for me to have a perfectly successful life. I was the daughter of a preacher then eventually married a preacher. Perfect, huh?

REWIND.

The real deal is that my Daddy preached for a string of small churches in various states, so rather than living in a sheltered and secure environment to nurture my confidence, we moved so much I was always the "new kid" at school. I was an introvert and insecure and invisible, but I was a perfectionist.

Despite my childhood I sought the perfect quest to find the perfect mate and have 2.5 children to grow up in my perfectly-kept dream house.

REWIND…AGAIN.

Instead of attending the university I had planned to attend in nearby Portland, Oregon, my Dad and I had an argument about my 11:30 p.m. curfew—even after graduation from high school—so I made a decision.

In a momentary fit of non-perfect irrational thinking, I told him I wanted to go to school in Texas. I was thinking rather than a couple of hundred miles away, I wanted to put a thousand miles of distance so I could have my freedom. Plus, I finally realized the chances of my hooking up with my junior high and high school heartthrob would never happen since he really did seem to think I was invisible.

So, my envisioned perfect escape to Texas for my perfect freedom was perfectly devastating. My daddy put me on a Greyhound Bus for a long (emphasis on long) three-day journey to a small town 35 miles southeast of Dallas.

Imagine, if you would, this scared eighteen-year-old, first time ever away from home, being dropped off at a dinky, rickety building, which served as the town's bus terminal. Plus, it was in the '70's, and I was in the South. So when a man with a southern drawl, unfamiliar to my Seattle-bred ears, asked me, "Yu lookin for tha colored school?" I could not even form an answer. Apparently, the only Black people that came to town via the bus, came to attend the town's only Black college, so he called to have me picked up.

Within minutes (everything was in minutes then) a rusted, faded blue and white van pulled up with the letters SWCC barely legible. Leroy (how perfectly suited for my driver to have that name) drove me as I began to dream of a perfectly beautiful and quaint college on acres of beautifully landscaped, rolling meadows.

REWIND.

We "crossed" the tracks and I found myself on the grounds of Southwestern Christian College, all of which I could see in the one spot where I stood. Leroy informed me that the girls' dormitory wasn't quite ready so until then, I would be staying with a few other girls under Dean Franklin's care. (That is another story).

Leroy set my trunk just a few feet from the railroad tracks (which I grew to realize you could set your watch by this accurate, consistent, and hourly passing) in front of a dilapidated house I had to share with six other girls. We only had two rooms and one bathroom. Of course, we were outnumbered by mice, roaches, and mosquitoes!

With my newest perfect dream dashed, I began a new quest, to plead, beg and cajole my daddy to let me come home. After using all my coins in the pay phone, my daddy stopped accepting my collect calls.

After three days of sulking and isolating , I finally resigned myself to my far from imagined fate. So on that third night, I heard the usual singing as I had the two previous nights. Later I discovered that there was nothing else to do but sing! The students would gather on the steps of the administration building, which face the campus' centerpiece, a big grassy circle.

With my perfect dream faded, I ventured out into the star-lit, humid dark night and I made out the silhouette of someone sitting off from the other students on the curb right on the grassy circle. I asked the silhouette if I could sit there. The reply came, "It's a free curb."

The silhouette ended up being my spouse of forty years and counting, but after those first cocky words, I should have done like was told to Forrest Gump, "Run Forrest, Run!"

For that silhouette was not that perfect mate I was destined to have. Yet after those days of crying enough tears to end California's drought and having my perfect dream shattered, I was grasping for anything at that point.

Turns out, that in the light of day, "silhouette" was not half bad. He was not tall, and dark, like my perfect mate should have been, was handsome and but he beat my 5'2" by 5" and was a nice, sweet honey, caramel color and could sing.

He sported a big Afro too. Keep in mind I still did not fit in well with my surroundings and my Seattle lifestyle and way of talking stood out. So "Big Afro" wanted to change me from what he called an "Oreo" cookie to a "double fudge" cookie. Later he told me he also liked my

fat knees, which were emphasized when I wore my perfectly matched knee high, socks with my jumpers and turtleneck sweaters.

As we planned a future to my dismay, I soon learned he did not share my perfect dream of a beautiful home or owning a business (I had always dreamed of owning a preschool).

Once again, my perfectly planned dream shattered and to add to my misery, of all the things he could have chosen to do in life…what did he choose? He decided to become a youth pastor, eventually a preacher. *Oh where was my perfect life?*

Instead of a beautiful suburban home in a pristinely kept neighborhood of finely manicured lawns, we lived in "the hood" of Los Angeles, directly across from the church building. Instead of having a beautifully decorated home, that could be the envy of any on "HGTV" my husband insisted we live a "down to earth" lifestyle and that a house was for "living" not a museum showpiece for display only.

I wanted a perfect place with a place for everything and everything in its place. He wanted everything anywhere and no particular place for anything.

Even with the planning of our children…you know the United States national average of 2.5 (the .5 is really a dog) we ended up with .5 over or in other words, three children. All of our attempts to have a pet dog were so far from my perfect dream, it would take another story; "Diary of the Family who Couldn't Keep a Dog,"

In my perfect world, child number one was supposed to be a son. Well, you guessed it, we had a daughter. Yet we put a perfect plan together for her arrival. Took Lamaze classes, and rehearsed "D" day (delivery day). I was given a Christmas date for my due date and after numerous occasions of false labor and rushing to UCLA hospital, I finally became so accustomed to the sensations in my abdomen that I just ignored them.

So, on a Wednesday night, late in January, I enjoyed a huge meal one of the sisters from church provided for me before she went to Bible class. I had so much energy after eating, that I cleaned and mopped my kitchen and cleaned the house to my perfection. I worked all through the ever-increasing sensations in my abdomen.

By the time my husband returned at 9 p.m. those "sensations" could no longer be ignored. Yet, I did not have much conviction when I told my husband because now, after so much false labor, I really thought I had a false pregnancy or would simply be pregnant forever. My husband called UCLA hospital, and after hearing the frequency of my "sensations which now I knew were full blown contractions, we were told to come to the hospital immediately. My husband suddenly got so nervous he got on the freeway going in the wrong direction even though we had rehearsed numerous times.

Well, by the time we got to the hospital, I was whisked straight to the delivery room, no time for the usual prep. Then we were told even though I was fully dilated, the baby had not dropped at all and was in distress. I would have to have a Cesarean (C-section). I cried and said "NO, we have to do it the Lamaze way!"

They booted my husband out but then suddenly the nurse shouted "the baby is coming now!"

Well, they rushed to get my husband and he arrived seconds before his first born swooshed out...along with the remains of my huge meal! UGu!! (the doctor said another word that I cannot use).

Well, the nurse, (the same one I clawed when fighting not to have a C-section) cleaned up the infant, and I cried. Of course my husband thought they were tears of joy but I was looking at the little alien-looking creature that had come out of me and was wondering why my husband was cooing "she's so beautiful!" He and that little creature are still bonded to this day.

There was more drama two years later when the first son came and I should have ended it then…since I had a boy and girl now, but NO, deviating from my perfect plan, two years after our first son comes another.

The five of us lived years in that small house in "the hood". One of the more perfect aspects was that I never lacked an available babysitter. The teens loved our kids. My daughter, now a mother of two, cannot believe her "perfectionist" mother allowed so many people to babysit especially since she is so extremely cautious regarding her children. Of course times are different.

It seems everything I had dreamed that would be perfect for my perfectionist persuasion ended up the complete opposite. Instead of owning a preschool, using my gift of patience to nurture children, I have been with DMV years listening to 'grown" people cry and whine about their driver licenses and car registrations.

None of my children took up my desires to have "a place for everything." They took after their Dad. Yet, in spite of my imperfect college choice, non-perfect mate, imperfect children, imperfect career, I can echo the words of a Biblical character whose life changed suddenly on a Damascus road. Instead of living his dream life, he was persecuted, shipwrecked, jailed and beaten. Yet, he said he was content.

I would not trade any of my life-changing experiences at my Alma mater Southwestern

Christian College, nor meeting my "silhouette" soul-mate nor my uniquely gifted children each of whom I proudly brag about constantly. Even more "brag worthy" are my four perfect grandchildren that I perfectly adore and I am positive are the most perfect children ever born. Of course I am the perfect 'Nana' to my perfect angels. Well gotta go now. I am about plan for my "perfect" retirement.

Rubye Ellen Crigler has had a love for reading even as a child. Hiding from five siblings was the only way to enjoy a good book without interruption. Now reading is still a favorite past time as she resides in her San Fernando Valley home. She is proud mother of one daughter, two sons and extremely proud of two beautiful granddaughters and two handsome grandsons. Currently planning to retire at the end of 2014, she hopes at that time to start writing her very first book.

Diary of a Smiling Mom

By Primrose Cameron

Dear Diary,

The message is in the smile. My son hasn't always had a mustache, beard and deep voice. There used to be a time when he wanted me to pick out his clothes and pack his bag with snacks, or the earlier days when he depended on me for everything. Well, one thing has never changed— that smile. Got to love that smile. It may have a new meaning now, but I definitely understand where it comes from. It is a connection that we have always had.

Now that my son has entered his first year of college, we are able to continue to share the humorous days of his youth. Thank goodness he has a sense of humor because I was able to share these stories at his high school graduation. The sad part is, they all have to do with the bathroom, or lack thereof. I will never forget rushing home from a long day at college myself to be greeted by that unforgettable two-year-old smile. For the life of me I couldn't remember when we had attempted to put him in big boy underwear, but I thought, *Thank goodness it finally happened, he's potty trained.*

Who had time to worry about that any way? I was so glad to be home and to have him in my arms. We went off to do our daily routine of playing with educational toys and learning letters and numbers (he has always been my scholar). But for some reason, the mother in me was curious, so I asked, "When did he start wearing big boy underwear?"

His communication was, of course, limited. But he did flash that smile, which could've meant any number of things. *Mommy I had a great day. Mommy I missed you, Mommy, what are we doing next?* But this particular day would be a hide and seeks kind of day. The only problem was that he wasn't hiding and I had no clue what I was seeking.

That was until it hit me. Literally. I sniffed the air. "Did someone forget to take out the trash?" I said.

As my son began to giggle, I gave him that *What did you do face?* The more he giggled, the more concerned I became. As if he knew what I was thinking, he began pulling me by the hand into his room. I knew that the garbage could not have moved into his room, so the search was on. I looked in the closet, while he giggled. I looked under the bed, while he giggled. And then, I looked in the dresser drawer with his big boy underwear, while he giggled. There it was... his pull-up (that should have been in the trash). This child had changed from his pull-ups into underwear with a smile. Got to love that smile!

The next story should have really come first, but I really think it was more my fault than his. I could never figure out what the smile meant without words. This particular day we were grocery shopping. My son had to have been under two years old (pre-potty trained) as I pushed him in the cart. He was always known to be a happy baby, full of smiles and giggles. I couldn't wait until he was able to do things on his own like a big boy, but at this point he was my grocery shopping teammate and no matter what I said, he thought that I was funny. We made it through the last needed isle, cashed out and were ready to go. Then it hit me, something was not right. Did this grocery store forget to take out the trash? Was the produce no good? I looked in my basket to see my son smiling, then giggling. All I could think was, *Why did I put him in shorts? Why wasn't the pull-up working? What was I going to tell the manager of the store? What was I going to do with this cart?*

I went in immediate mother mode. I grabbed the giggling baby, told the store clerk I was sorry and I ran out of there while balancing bags. This child was still smiling, while I was trying to escape. You have to love that smile.

I have learned so many heartfelt lessons from being able to parent a boy toward manhood. Most importantly, I have learned to communicate with my son in a variety of ways and I know that there are times when no words are needed and his smile says it all

His elementary school years were a blast. Lessons learned took place daily for him and me. When he was in second grade, (as I taught ninth graders), my son decided that he was going to protect his toy soldier instead of being engaged in his lessons at school. For a good part of the school day, I received emails that informed me that my son spent most of his day walking over to his backpack after each question or statement, telling his teacher, "I will only be a minute."

This would have not been a problem, if it really was only a minute. The minutes added up and could not be replaced and of course, he did it all with a smile. The teacher told me that she hated bothering me because he was such a good kid and she loved his smile. Now what did this smile mean? *Did he think that it was okay to not listen? Did he really feel that his toy would not be safe without him? Wait a minute, why did he bring a toy to school?* Fortunately for me, when it was time for me to pick him up from school, he wore the same smile that I left him with in the morning and the same one that he shared with the teacher throughout the day. I kindly asked him how his day went and enthusiastically, he said it was great and he did so much in school.

With my own smile, I asked him for his toy soldier and shared with him that his toy wouldn't be able to go to school anymore. He probably had choice words to share with me (second grade language of course), but with a smile he nodded and with a smile he was ready for the next day at school.

The best part of being a mother is that the game may change, but your title doesn't. There is something special about hearing your son rename you: mommy, mother, mom, and ma. I absolutely love it. I can't say that he has always agreed, but he has always acknowledged the current situation. The message that he is interested in sharing with me is always in the smile, or lack thereof left for interpretation.

What I have learned from being a mother is that it is very important to communicate with our children despite the hard decisions that must be made. They will not always agree nor appreciate it at that current moment, but they will be able to reflect and know that what we do for them is all out of love.

My son is no longer the cute little kid, who hides his pull-ups, but he is now the young adult who has pulled himself up and that's a great feeling, knowing that I had something to do with his success.

Although there may be bumpy roads, I am willing to help steer the car because I know that he was built for greatness.

In college, the instructors are not emailing me when he looks into his backpack but because the channel of communication that was created at birth, I know how he is doing. He actually shares his success with me. He has always shared something— whether good or bad. I have never had a manual to do this thing called parenting, but I have definitely had continuous lessons learned through trial and error. Whether it was the way I tried to teach him to tie his shoe, or how I tried to assist him with middle school math (I wasn't quite successful at that), at least I know that I tried.

I can no longer carry him in my arms nor do I choose his clothes for the next school day, but I definitely am able to communicate with my one and only son. He will tell you that I don't always get it and there may need to be a few more attempts made, but with his smile (and mine) we make it through any situation. And of course his smiles are sometimes frowns or sideway grins, but we are communicating.

Nineteen years later and I still get hugs and kisses on the cheek, but I am very thankful that I am not in a position to have to run out of the grocery store or check the dresser drawers for accidents. The messages are in the smile and you have to love that smile!

Dr. Primrose Cameron is the mother of one son, who is currently a first year college student. She lives in Florida.

Diary of a Faithful Mom

By Naleighna Kai

My son, J. L., stood in the middle of the empty one-bedroom apartment. He glanced around, then frowned before telling the property manager, "I'm not impressed."

She was a little taken aback by him. He was seventeen at the time. She was showing him the apartment because he made the appointment and went to see the place on his own, even after I told him that I couldn't afford to move into that building. She took him to another place. When he was done looking around there, he said, "I'm still not impressed."

She took him to yet another place. When he scanned the area; swept through each of the rooms, he smiled at her and said, "*This* is my mother's new apartment."

Now, mind you, brother-man did not have a job. He was preparing to go off to college in a few weeks, and he was making moves that were *waaaay* above my pay grade. At the time, we lived in a place called Princeton Park Homes—an area of homes in Chicago built near the Dan Ryan

Expressway. Some nights, we slept on the floor because the gunshots were something fierce.

Eventually, I made the decision that if there was a bullet with my name on it, it could meet me on the floor, too. I started sleeping in my comfortable bed from that point on. But my son, who was on his way to Fisk on a presidential scholarship, had said, "Mom, I'm not going to be able to keep my mind on school, knowing that you're still living here."

So, he—of the 'I'm seventeen and school is my focus' clan—set out to find me a better place to live. I only know the intimate details of what transpired between him and the property manager, because the woman, whose name was JoAnn, called me at work and told me every single move my son had made in his visit to the building, then said, "Your son is amazing."

I thought, *Well, tell me something I don't know.*

But hey, it was her call, and I wasn't sure why she was on the other end of my line in the first place. I had already told her that I wouldn't be able to move into her building.

JoAnn said, "You know, I have people on the waiting list for this apartment. I have people who have a deposit on this particular apartment; but if you want it, it's yours."

I did a mental sweep of my finances. Deposit, security, moving costs— and came up snake eyes. Hell, when I told her I wasn't moving in, I had immediately paid next month's rent in the spot where we currently lived. So I was on empty!

"JoAnn, I would love the place, but right now, it's not looking too good."

"You son seems to think otherwise," she replied. "Think about it, then call me back and let me know."

My son came home, all happy until I gave him the bad news that I couldn't take the apartment. He quickly said, "Mom, you were the one who talks about having faith. Did yours go on vacation?"

Well, dang. What a way to say that.

"Two years ago, when you looked at my grades, you didn't think I would get into college, right?"

"Right," I replied, remembering the ton of horrible grades that were the mainstay of his freshman and sophomore year. The only good grades he received were in band and lunch!

"But where am I going to be next month?" he asked, one eyebrow raised.

"The school you fell in love with on the college tour."

"Exactly. Fisk University. And I what I did a couple of years ago didn't matter, it's what I believed could happen."

For a year, he had been claiming, "Thank you, Lord, my college costs are paid in full at little or no cost to me or my mother."

On the college tour, he had given the admissions director a copy of his book that was published when he was sixteen. They asked my son to come speak for their Talented Tenth event in Nashville, and when he was done, they gave him a scholarship that was very close to what he had been affirming. So, despite what his grades looked like; despite what I thought—my son was on his way to college. If there was anyone that could teach me about Faith—it was him.

His visit and little pep talk to me were on Wednesday. I received another call that evening. One of my former clients, who I helped with getting two of their books finished, wanted me to slide by her house in the morning. *Morning?* Back then, I wasn't a morning person. I wasn't an afternoon person. (As quiet as it's kept, I wasn't an evening person either! But I digress). This woman wanted me to come to her place before work because she needed to speak with me.

"Mom, you should go see, Ms. Betty," my son told me as I complained about the early morning request.

Oooookay— cab time, then bus time, and get-to-work on time. I was at her place in Jackson Park Highlands early that morning and it was the fastest meeting in the world. She simply slid an envelope my way and said, "I really appreciate all you've done for me. And I just wanted to say thank you."

That envelope contained enough cash for the first month's rent in the new apartment (which was double the rent of the current one I lived in). Baby, you can thank me with Benjamins anytime you see fit. To say I did a happy dance all the way to the bus stop was putting it mildly. (It was probably more like the Electric Slide, or some other complicated dance, but I was elated). I had never charged her a consultant fee for doing her books; and she became my mentor, almost like a fourth mother.

I called JoAnn when I got to work and said, "I have some cash in my hot little hands. It's enough for the first month, but I still don't have the security just yet."

JoAnn said, "We don't normally do this …" (Don't you LOVE when sentences start that way?) "But I'll spread the security over several months. We'll tack on an additional $100 per month until it's paid. You'll sign a separate promise to pay document. How does that sound?"

My son's words echoed in my head. *Faith.* "Sounds like I'll be taking the apartment. Thank you soooo very much."

"You can move in on Saturday."

"Saturday? But that's two days from now."

"Yes, but it's ready," she said. "And I have some guys who'll help you move if you *need them.*"

Done deal!!!

I gave my son the good news and he smiled and said, "Remember what the sermon was this past Sunday?"

On that Sunday prior to this call, my minister at the time, Sesvalah, had talked about "taking God out of the box." *The same energy you use to ask God for a two-room shack is the same energy that God can use to supply you a mansion. The same energy you use to ask God to supply you with a Hooptie, is the same one He can slide you into a BMW.* (Seriously? Where they do that?). The week before, I had already told the woman I wasn't going to be moving in. But just like my son had done for college, I took the message seriously and started thanking the Creator for my new two-bedroom, two-bathroom, deluxe apartment with a balcony, all appliances, and an excellent view of Lake Michigan and Downtown Chicago. With my son's encouragement, I started thanking the Creator that I already had it. But going by my finances, there was no way that I could have moved into that place. No way! Putting it out there made my angels, ancestors, teachers, and guides move into action, got them off the Bid Whist tournament they were holding, and started them on coordinating things so that my desire could be met. Even when I felt that it couldn't happen, my son held the vision for me— held it strong enough that the property manager was moved by his faith.

The sermon was on Sunday. I started claiming on Monday. J. L saw the apartment on Wednesday. I visited Betty on Thursday. I put in the first month's rent, signed the lease and arranged the movers on Thursday. I was in my new two-bedroom, two-bathroom, deluxe apartment in Oglesby Towers with Lake Michigan and Downtown Chicago views on Saturday.

I won't mention that when I called the place where I lived at the time and mentioned that I was moving out immediately that they said to send them a letter dated for 30 days prior stating that I was moving out. They gave me every single dime of my current rent and my deposit back. No, I won't mention that. I also won't mention that JoAnn never did that required credit check (because at that time it would have been laughable if she had).

I won't mention that I lost my job two weeks after I moved in. I won't mention that I never missed making a rent payment in the seven years that I lived there. I won't mention that the only reason that I finally moved from that beautiful place was because the building, after 35 years, was sold and the vibe of the building, as well as the new people that were moving into it, changed drastically. I won't mention that the new property manager switched to a new job, and made sure that I slid into the new building she managed on a month-to-month— all with the thought that I would be moving into a new house at some time soon.

No, I won't mention any of that because that would seem like everything was too much of a coincidence. And that the little seed of faith, planted by my son, helped to sprout into an orchard of lessons in strength, determination and allowing the Creator to direct the flow of my life.

My son continues to inspire me, even to this day. He didn't manage to pull the straight A's needed to maintain that scholarship, but he, too, learned a series of lessons that helped fashion him into a man who believes that God has his back. A year after having to leave Fisk to go to work, his job in Nashville ended and he was forced to make the trek back home to Chicago and to another series of lessons. That wonderful apartment he shifted me into became a little "too comfortable" for a young man who was always about handling his business. And for a moment, he wasn't making himself the priority. Everything and everyone came before him.

Well, mama did what she felt best at the time and shook up the nest. Soon, having an "address" became top priority—which means he became his first priority—as it should be. Finishing what he started—getting that degree, getting to that place where he could sustain himself as a unit whether I was here to experience it or on Spirit side watching over him.

Months later, he was still a little angry with me. My actions on "shifting him out of the nest" had caused the first rift ever in our relationship. I felt really saddened by it, but as a mother, I was afraid of becoming the kind of mother who enabled a young man to a point where he did not reach his full potential. So while it saddened me, I truly believed I did the right thing.

Well, I was the one to give my son a housewarming for his new apartment that he managed to snag within a mere two months of leaving the nest. All of sudden, between school, the part-time job, paying the bills, and having very little money left over, I believe the message finally sank in—he needed to get his butt back in school, needed to handle his business and get more in line with what he wanted to do: teach, have a wife, children, a home—a life.

That fall, I hired my son to be the disc jockey for a literary event that I give each year in Chicago. While he was there, a man walked in with one of my sponsors. I recognized him immediately as the man in a picture that my son took on the college tour many years ago. This was the only other person who my son gave his book to—at the time he was the admissions director for Alabama A&M, another one of the schools on the five-city Southern tour. He had since moved on to become the admissions director for South Carolina State University.

As he embraced my son, I said, "My son would really like to go back to school."

The man whipped out a business card and placed it in my son's hand. That next week, my son was on top of everything needed to apply. Two months later, he was on a plane to South Carolina and enrolled into the university there. A few months later, that admissions director took a job elsewhere, but my son is still there, has landed a scholarship every semester after that first one. The latest merit scholarship covered tuition, a meal plan, and books. He'll be finishing up within a year of this writing.

If there is one thing I love about being a mother, it that my son teaches me in words and deeds about exercising my faith muscle. And sometimes, in words and deeds, it is our job to help them to remember about exercising their own.

Naleighna Kai is the national bestselling author of Every Woman Needs a Wife, with a spin-off titled, The Pleasure's All Mine and the controversial new novel, Open Door Marriage. She is the mother of J. L. Woodson, the NAACP Image Award nominee for Outstanding Literature. Naleighna started writing in December of 1999, independently publishing her first two novels before acquiring a book deal with an imprint of Simon & Schuster and most recently a book deal with Brown Girl Publishing.

Naleighna is the CEO of Macro Marketing & Promotions Group, the Director of Marketing & Promotions for Brown Girls Publishing, as well as the marketing consultant to several national bestselling and aspiring writers. She is also the brainchild behind the annual Cavalcade of Authors events, which takes place in her hometown of Chicago. Naleighna pens contemporary fiction, erotica, and speculative fiction and is currently working on her next novels.

Find her on the web at www.naleighnakai.com, www.thecavalcadeofauthors.com and on Facebook under Naleighna Kai.

Diary of a Mom Who Laughs A Lot

By Marcena Hooks

It is amazing how time brings about a change. I was a mom working full-time, relishing in the silence at work. Now, I am a listening mom, who stays at home and laughs out loud all the time, and who wouldn't trade in the golden moments of hearing the voices of my kids for anything.

My son, Terrynce (Tee), who is the youngest at age five, cracks me up the most. I really believe he has been here before. Questions he asks me like "Mom, when I am going to get hair under my pits?" (maybe he has seen his dad's armpit hair?) force me to answer him with an "I don't know. Maybe when you're older." Or when he asked "Why don't I get to use deodorant yet?" That was because he has seen his big sister put it on and has heard me remind her to use it. Brianna (Bri) is only seven, but after playing outside all day, she can get a little musty.

One day, he asked her "What's wrong, baby sister?"

His tone of voice really showed he cared and was interested. All Brianna did was sigh or do something semi-dramatic, but he thought she was really upset. This cracked me up so much because he is the youngest, smallest, shortest person in the house but has the biggest personality. His size and age don't mean a thing to him, and he is not going to play second fiddle to anyone or anything. He really thinks he's the boss!

Usually, the dramatic one is Brianna. One day, Terrynce was a little drama king. He yelled "Mom, I need a little help here!"

I rushed into the bathroom thinking maybe he had fallen in the toilet or was almost drowning in the tub. All he needed was help reaching the towel rack. Really son? I almost broke my neck running to get to him, thinking he was hurt, only to find out he was just being a little lazy.

Another funny moment in our lives was when we flew from Oklahoma to California. It was the first time for the kids and I must say, they were awesome on the plane ride. Brianna had a little trouble with her ears, but for the most part, it was a good flight for them. Terrynce was so amazed during takeoff, that he said, "Wow! Is this the whole earth?" to his dad as he looked out the window. See, he is a brave little boy and will try almost anything. I don't even like the window seat!

Brianna and Terrynce fight pretty much every day. They get in trouble for it every day. Bri doesn't understand that since she is the oldest, that her baby brother wants to do everything she does and more, and wants her to let him. He wants to be like her. I tell her this all the time. Terrynce doesn't understand that she is older and is a girl; he's a boy and they are just different. All of the explaining in the world does not stop them. Terrynce has jumped off one couch onto another, with his balled-up fist behind him, ready to hit Brianna in the face!

Luckily, my husband, Larry, saw it coming and saved Brianna as Terrynce was within inches of her jaw. Boy, did Terrynce get a beatdown that day.

We teach them not to fight, especially one another, and that they should share, love each other, and be nice to each other. Apparently, that goes in one ear and out the other.

One time, Bri told me that Tee hit her in her left nose hole. Very quickly I had to process what the heck she was talking about. When I realized it, I wanted to tell her it's called a nostril, but her seven-year-old description suited me.

The tables were turned when Bri got to Tee. He said "Mom, Bri hit me in the white part of my eye really hard." Eyeball would've sufficed, but again, why correct a four-year-old on this? His description is so much funnier. I don't bother to correct or change what he has to say most times unless it's really wrong.

Another time, I knew Bri hurt Tee was when I heard him howl a blood-curdling scream. Immediately, I went into protective mommy mode as I screamed back and asked him what happened. Mind you, I was in the bathroom where both children had been in out and out repeatedly. Tee proceeded to come in again and said, "Bri stepped on my foot like this." He showed me where as he lifted his foot and said she stepped on the bottom of it. "She's going to break every piece!"

Bri heard me laughing so hard that she had to come and be nosy. I told her the story and she said, "Well, he was in my way!"

One day in church, Brianna asked me is God invisible. I told her that He is physically, but that we can feel Him. I told her He lives inside of us. She proceeded to hit herself in the chest and said, "Uh-oh. I just punched him!" I had to laugh out loud in church. Brianna has a very creative imagination, and Tee is on his way.

Besides being funny, my kids can also hurt my feelings. I know they don't mean to, and most times don't know what they are really saying, but when they tell me they want another mommy because I am mean (only after I tell them no and they don't get their way, or give them a much-deserved whipping) that stings a little bit.

One time, I told Tee to go out and try to find him one. Then he asked, "What will happen to me out there?"

See, that's confirmation that he doesn't really mean it. I have to catch myself and remember that they are just kids. Most times, I ignore them when they say they want another mommy, and other times I go into my spiel about how much I love and care for them, how much they mean to me, and how everything I do and say, I have them and their well-being in mind. They just don't know! Plus when they tell me later in the same day that I am the best mom ever, well that certainly brightens up my day. I go from being the worst mom to the best mom in a matter of hours. Hey, I can certainly accept that!

My two crumb snatchers are really strong and have adapted to change really well. We have moved to a different state because of my husband's calling as a pastor. Bri and Tee have blended right in at church and school. It has taken me more time to adjust than them. In a way, I am grateful that they are young and more adaptable to change. They can easily make new friendships and start off fresh.

In our local church, we don't have children's church or child care. At least not yet. The kids have to sit with me. We have tried letting them sit with other members, but Larry has had to call out to them during his sermon and send them to sit with me. Times have changed in church as well. My kids are at the age where they have to be constantly entertained. I started out letting them play games on my old cell phone. Then they graduated to one of the members' iPad and cell phone. And yes, they knew passwords and codes, too. They would take turns with other kids and each other. I didn't approve of it at first, but it kept them quiet. They did find ways to fight over this too, and I always threatened that they got one chance and after that, all games would be off. I made good on my threatening promise more than once.

Their little necks should be sore and tired from holding their heads down during the entire church service. Larry changed from sending them to me, to giving praise for their quietness and still manner. He didn't have to wonder where they were or how they were acting. He could see them up front with me and that would ease his mind. That was until that same church mother who let them use her gadgets couldn't figure out what happened to her device. Apparently, Terrynce had downloaded an app and it did something to the phone. She couldn't retrieve her contact list and she was in a disarray, thinking she had lost all phone numbers! We tried everything after making Tee apologize, including turning the phone off and back on, and then removing and re-inserting the battery. The latter did the trick. What a relief! We still don't know what Terrynce did, but he won't have the chance to do it again. To this day, our kids are not allowed to use anyone else's electronic device. The solution? Samsung Galaxy 3 Kid Tablets for Christmas.

We have learned that kids will be kids, whether they are PKs (preacher's kids) or not. They are born smart and advanced even though they learn at different levels. Brianna has a lot to do with Terrynce's learning process in school; she is probably his best teacher. He looks up to her in more ways than one, and wants her approval. Brianna really is bossy, as she should be being the oldest, and does things to entice Terrynce. Every now and then he has to remind her that she is NOT the boss of him.

Their questions crack me up and I consider them nuggets. They are pivotal moments in my children's development. If I was working full-time, I'd miss a lot of these moments.

My diary title has changed from Working Mom to a Mom Who Laughs More. My kids literally make me LOL (Laugh Out Loud) and I wouldn't have it any other way.

God has given my husband and I two beautiful, brilliant, and healthy children. I couldn't ask for more. I am thankful for where the Lord has placed me right now in my life. It's right where I'm supposed to be.

Marcena Hooks is a stay-at-home mom who is married to a pastor. Originally from Oklahoma City, she and her family now reside in the Los Angeles, California area. They are the proud parents of two small children named Brianna (age 7) and Terrynce (age 5). Marcena can be reached at marcenac@yahoo.com.

Diary of a Stepmother

By NiaShanta McClellan Ross

"I'm gonna call CPS on you!" Jaila screeched.

"I'll call them for you! Want me to dial the number?" I yelled.

While that may have seemed like a scene from a drama-filled television show, it was actually a scene from my life.

How did two-thirds of the Ross union that stood at the altar twenty-four months prior filled with grins, hugs, and laughter, end up at this scene? It didn't happen overnight, but it was bound to happen.

Before getting to the nitty-gritty of that November night when my stepdaughter and I threw blows at one another, I've gotta give some background.

Being a stepmother was never a part of my plan; I always said that I would never date a guy with kids. (Craziest thing is, nearly all the guys I dated before getting married had kids. Go figure). I didn't want to deal with the baby-momma drama that most guys with kids had. I didn't want to have to deal with someone else's parenting style. Someone else's belief system. Someone else's kid. But, I've lived long enough to know that God could really care less about our wants. He gives us what He thinks we need. And that's exactly what I got with Miss Jaila Ross.

August 2011, a mere sixty days after jumping the broom, I found myself sitting across from Jaila's biological mother, her family, my husband, and an associate judge. Why? Because things had gone from bad to worse when it came to my stepdaughter. My husband, Jonathan, believed that Jaila was being neglected and wasn't receiving the care that she needed. It seemed that Jaila was being used as a pawn by her mother. Jonathan and Jaila's mom had been into it for years, and our nuptials only made things worse. So Jonathan and I petitioned for emergency custody of the then- nine-year-old, Jaila. After receiving temporary custody, my husband was still obligated to pay child support to her mother. Gotta love the great state of Texas, right?

So there we were, newlyweds-turned-full-time-parents to Jaila. According to the temporary orders, both parties (us and them—Jaila's mom and her boyfriend) had to prove that Jaila would be taken care of. Our attorney and their attorney worked together to come up with a visitation schedule. Home studies would also have to be performed to determine the best place for Jaila to live. Our temporary orders were good for a few months, and then, after the studies had been conducted, the judge would make a final ruling in the best interest of Jaila.

Meanwhile, we moved into a larger apartment, changed Jaila's school, and tried our best to make the transition as stress-free as possible for her. She took it very hard (as any child would) being taken from her mother's home, removed from her friends and the school that she had attended all of her life, and forced to live with her daddy and me—also known as "the foreigner."

Initially, things weren't so bad. Jaila's mom played the role. She called every night. She made sure Jaila was somewhat taken care of while at her home. She painted the picture that she was the ideal parent to the court, and tried her best to make us look like the worst parents on earth. Everyone (including the judge) knew that she was full of it, but there was one person that bought her exclusive brand of bologna—Jaila.

Whatever I did from that point on was wrong to Jaila. When I combed her hair, I had to constantly hear about how her mother did it better. I would slave over her full head of hair, only for her to take it down at school the next day. I would buy her clothes and have to hear about how her mom had better taste than me. Whatever I cooked wasn't good enough because it wasn't the same way her momma cooked. I had to explain why I was there and why her mother wasn't. I had to explain that I wasn't trying to take her mother's place or even be her momma. Those conversations went in one ear and out the other. I had to face it, the only woman that she wanted to see with her daddy was her momma. And no matter how much I tried to give her love, show her love, and even buy her love, she wasn't feeling it. Don't get me wrong, Jaila loved me and showed that she did, but I always felt like I was a substitute. A filler. A proxy until she could get to her momma.

We had our good days and our bad days. Days that I couldn't stand her and days that she couldn't stand me. After all, I hadn't signed up to be a momma. At least not a stepmother. But it was what it was. Technically, I did sign up for it when Ross became my new last name. Sure I knew when I said "I do" I'd have to do the whole stepmother thing, but full-time? That wasn't the plan. The plan was to be kid-free (primarily) until Jonathan and I had our own kids. Kids that I would birth. That sounds horrible, right? But that was my thought process. I thought I would have time to actually enjoy being married before being thrust into a full-fledge mother role.

Fast forward to the evening in question. We had been appointed Jaila's custodial parents in September 2012, although she had lived with us almost exclusively even before then. We had a routine and Jaila knew it. We knew. Everybody knew it. It was one that worked for us, or so I thought.

That evening started off like any other day. I had gone to work as did my husband and mom (who had been living with us for almost two years, but that's a whole 'nother book), and Jaila had gone to school. After we all got home, my husband and I were in the living room watching a recorded episode of *Real Housewives of Atlanta*, my mom was in her room watching TV, and Jaila was supposed to be in her room working on homework and an upcoming project.

She had come home with an attitude about something (as most twelve year olds do) and had had a stank 'tude all evening. At one point, she strutted through the living room and I asked her if she had finished her homework. Let her tell it, she had. I then asked her if she was working on the project that I had spent my last ten dollars on, and that little angel had the nerve to get fly with me. *Hood translation: to "get fly" means to (1) to lose one's mind temporarily, (2) to exert a certain type of power that is non-existent, etc., derived from the phrase "She got fly with me when I asked her something."*

I asked again if she had finished her project and she rolled her eyes, asked my husband and I, "Why are y'all in my business," and then had the audacity to storm off down the hallway, mumbling some sort of gibberish under her breath.

Let's pause for a moment to regain our composure. *Woooo-saaaa....woooo-saaaa.* I'm getting mad all over again recalling this story, and I'm sure you're feeling some type of way reading it. Kids today have lost their minds. And she had definitely lost her mind that evening.

As Jaila stomped her pre-adolescent self down the hallway, my husband and I turned to look at one another. He looked at me. I looked at him. We paused the TV, and plotted out our next move. My husband, all 6'3," 400 plus pounds of him wanted to march down the hallway and let her knew what time it was, but I informed him that I would handle it. I usually had a better way of dealing with her. Jonathan didn't do much talking. He talked with his belt. And seeing as how

Jaila was 5'4" tall, she and I were close enough in height to see eye-to-eye, literally. I figured it would be another one of those times when she talked, I talked, we talked, and then we came to an understanding. Man, was I wrong.

When I walked into her room, she was standing up next to her bed, noticeably annoyed. I asked her what her problem was, but she didn't answer. Instead, she shook her head. I asked her again what was wrong with her. She still remained silent. I told her that I would ask her one more time, but she didn't seem phased. She kept that same stupid look on her face like she was running the house, and I was her kid.

She had me twisted.

I walked up to her, stood nose to nose with her, and asked her again what her problem was and what she had mumbled under her breath as she exited the living room.

Jaila had the nerve to say to me, "If I so-called said something, what did I say?" Then the little angel had the nerve to roll her eyes and look away from me.

I snapped.

The next thing I knew, we had fallen onto her bed, tussling like two sisters fighting over clothes. She grabbed my hair. I grabbed hers. She cursed at me. I cursed at her. It was on like Donkey Kong! We struggled for what seemed like an eternity. She was out of breath. I was out of breath. She was tired. I was dog-tired.

The next words that I heard were from my momma in the next room over. "Jonathan, go in that room before they kill each other!"

Jaila yanked at my hair again and I did the same to her. "Get off of me," she yelled. "I'm gonna call CPS on you."

I grabbed the phone from the other side of the room, clearly out of breath and shouted, "I will call the number for you!"

The next thing I knew, my husband of a few short years and the father of the demon child (because she surely was no angel now) emerged. As he entered the room, I stood near the doorframe, and cried uncontrollably.

My momma soon came in to make sure that I was okay, and that Jaila was okay, too. Jonathan hugged me and told me that he loved me. He also assured me that everything would be fine, and that it was just a matter of time before me and Jaila had it out. He then told me and momma to step out for a minute so that he could talk to Jaila.

For the rest of the night, I wondered what my fate would be. I wondered if I would be jailed. I wondered if I would be punished. I wondered if I would be a divorcee'. I wondered if Jaila hated me. Wondered if she still loved me. I wondered if she would go to her uppity school the next day and tell her uppity teachers that her abusive stepmother assaulted her. I wondered if she was really going to call CPS. I wondered if I would have to show her momma what time it was after she found out. I'm not gonna lie. I prayed harder than I had prayed in a while that night.

The next day I was scheduled to attend an in-service for my job. I spent the majority of the day worrying. *What had I done to deserve all of this?* I ate all my vegetables as a kid. I tithed—not like I was supposed to,—but I did. I had accepted a child that wasn't mine from day one. I had put my entire marriage on the back-burner to make sure Jaila had what she needed.

I can sort of laugh at this story now, but there was nothing funny about what went down in that room that night. I know for a fact that the both of us took whatever opportunity we could to hurt the other person. I broke my nail going upside her head, but it also broke my heart to know that things had gotten that bad between us. She hadn't seen or heard from her mother in months, had recently started middle school, and was going through all types of emotional and physical changes. I had been through an unbelievable amount of work and financial stress, had been arguing frequently with my husband about the relationship between Jaila and I, and I had been dealing with all the court proceedings and drama. I thought drama dropped off after marriage, but mine slapped me in the face before the ink dried on my marriage license. Money had been tight trying to afford a "luxury" apartment so that Jaila could attend the best school in Plano, TX, and she had the audacity to jump stupid with me? *("Jump stupid" is a synonym of "jumping fly." See definition above.)*

Since that infamous November evening, Jaila and I have had a much better relationship. We aren't best friends (not that I think parents and their kids need to be friends), but we have a good relationship considering all that has transpired. Her momma still chooses to be a parent when it is convenient for her. Jaila and I talk more and really work on maintaining a mother-daughter relationship.

Blended families are something else. There is no manual on how to make them work. Sometimes they work wonderfully, and other times it's like pulling teeth. I am absolutely not an expert on blended families, but there is one thing I know for sure: communication is the key. There were times that my husband felt like he was in the middle of a catty feud between two crazy, emotional women. There were times that he didn't consider me or my feelings. Had we communicated, things would have been different. If Jaila and I communicated more/better, maybe things would have never gotten as bad as they did.

I have mad respect for woman who are stepmothers. I think it is way harder than just being a parent. You have to deal with the ex and their family, the family you married into (who always have an opinion about how you should handle the child), and the spouse (who is torn between the person they vowed to love and cherish, and the child they created). I'm doing as good a job as I know how, and I dare someone to come for me. I bet one thing is for sure: Jaila Ross won't come for me unless I send for her.

In the words of the late, great Tupac Shakur, "I ain't a killer, but don't push me."

NiaShanta McClellan-Ross is a native Oklahoman, born and raised in Tulsa. After receiving her BA in English and

MS in education from Southern University and Oklahoma State University respectively, NiaShanta moved to Dallas, TX to pursue one of her greatest passions: teaching. She currently teaches American Literature in a suburb outside of Dallas, TX. NiaShanta lives with her husband, mother, and stepdaughter in Plano, TX. She enjoys reading, cooking, and writing Inspirational Fiction.

Diary of an Almost Teen Mom

By Kay Alizeti

When I was 18, my closest friends and I discovered that I was the only one of the four of us who was still on the island...that is...still a virgin. It was then that I decided, "What the heck! There's no need to wait for marriage. My friends didn't." Peer pressure is a beast.

So, instead of holding on to my virginity like an Olympic gold medal, I ended up squandering it with the first man I was alone with. Thus began my "sex life".

I had only been intimate with one other person when I discovered I was pregnant from my then sixteen-year-old boyfriend. He'd originally told me he was nineteen. Naïve does not begin to describe the eighteen-year-old me. I missed my period and thought nothing of it until my mother started asking me about it. I was a high school senior at the top of my class. Surely, I should have known that it was a problem. Imagine my surprise when my mom carted me off to the doctor one morning before school.

At my pediatrician's office, I was given the cup…you know the one…they want your urine. When he told me that I was pregnant, I had no idea what was about to happen. He told me that I had "options." *What the heck did that mean*, I wondered. One of the options he told me about was abortion. I hadn't a clue of what that really meant. I mean, I knew the dictionary definition, but I was sure that I didn't want to do that. My mother made it clear what she wanted when we got in the car though.

She asked, "So what are you gonna do?" I swear I saw fangs peeking from under her lips.

Tears skidded down my face and interrupted my voice when I responded, "I guess I have no choice but to have it."

As dark as my mother is, I swear she turned red and steam came from her ears. "Oh, yes you do have a choice! You are getting rid of that!"

I could have sworn she said that I had a choice. She had made up my mind for me. I was terrified to tell her that it was not the choice I had made nor wanted. I had heard stories about abortion and that you were killing a baby. I simply didn't have it in me to tell my mother that I did not want to do that.

The way I figured, I could still graduate and maybe not even show. After all, it was March. Graduation was only three months away. I could continue working my job at the fast food restaurant and figure out a way to go to school part-time. The way my mom figured, though, I was going to graduate with honors and get my butt into somebody's college. I'd already been accepted into one that was about an hour and a half away from home and I was already enrolled in a local college while I finished high school. So, that was not a big issue. I guess she figured, she was done raising babies since my youngest sibling was thirteen years old then.

I cried for hours after she told me my decision. To add insult to injury, I had to make my own appointment. Because I was eighteen and technically an adult, she couldn't make it for me. That was another opportunity to say no to my mother. She glared at me as she pointed to the words I was supposed to say to the lady on the phone. I just knew she hated me. It showed all over her face. There, in her sight, I made an appointment for one week later to terminate my pregnancy.

The ride to the clinic was horrific. The closest one to our town was an hour and a half away from us. I sat in the car listening to my mom fuss about how irresponsible I was. Then, angry silence filled the car. She was disgruntled for having to take me, which I understood, but at the same time, I couldn't understand why she was mad at me when *she* was the one who told me that I was going.

When we got to the clinic, I was surprised to see that it just looked like a normal doctor's office or similar to what I've come to know as an urgent care center. There were no protesters outside. There were no bushes or trees around to hide anyone who might be waiting to take me out as I walked in to end the life that had begun to grow inside of me. It was just a regular old run-of-the-mill medical facility.

I walked in behind my mom with my head hung low. I remember thinking that I was a disgrace to my family. Never mind the fact that both my mother and grandmother were teenage mothers. I was somehow the one who had done this horrible thing to my family. Surely no one loved me anymore. What kind of example was I setting for my younger sister? Did she know what was happening? My brain just would not settle down.

Inside the building, it was bright and cheerful but cold and disconnected. The walls were pastel yellow but the posters on the wall were scary. There were different stages of pregnancy and descriptions of what was going on at each stage. When they called my number for me to go to the back, I froze in my seat. It was all at once very real that I was pregnant and I was about to end it. My mother's finger tapping my shoulder thawed my feet and allowed me to move toward the person calling my number.

The colors changed and everything was stark white. I started to wonder if I was now going to be cleansed of my sin. The long hallway had doors on either side that were closed. Soft cries could be heard and in one room a loud argument was being had. My escort quickened her pace to get me to the room where I would wait for the doctor.

I was told that I would have an ultrasound to determine if I was the right gestational age for the procedure. They said I was about eight weeks pregnant, then proceeded to show me what types of things were happening as the baby developed. They sent a counselor in to make sure I understood what was about to happen. She explained the entire procedure and asked me if I was sure this was what I wanted. She even asked if I was forced to make the decision. Her final question caused me to pause but I answered in a way that allowed the procedure to be continued. I felt like God was giving me one last chance to change my mind. I punked out, though, because I was afraid of my mom. I was also afraid to have to be homeless with a baby on the way because surely, my mom would put me out if I defied her.

The doctor came in and with few words began the procedure. I don't know what he said or didn't say because all I heard was the gurgling and whirring of the machine he controlled. It was the thing that was sucking the budding life from my body. That was the moment I decided that I never wanted to have children. I didn't want to have to go through this type of thing again. I felt so violated.

Unfortunately, that experience is what began my promiscuity. For the next six years, I was looking for love under and over most men I encountered. My dad was rarely around when I was a kid. The way my mom handled my pregnancy at eighteen made me think that she did not love me. That left me looking for it in all the wrong places. As smart as I was (or am), I could not make myself believe that I was loved by anyone. False promises, compliments, gifts and mediocre sexual intercourse translated to love as far as I could see.

At twenty-four, I found myself pregnant again. This time, I was out from my mother's rule and I had to make the decision on my own. I consulted the father, who had been so in love with me up until the minute I said I was pregnant. He suddenly wasn't ready for kids. His suggestion? "Get rid of it." He would pay for it. I felt like I could finally stand up to someone on this issue and I did. I let him know that whether he chose to participate or not, that year, he would have a child on this earth.

One rock down and one to go, I finally told my mother who lived 200 miles away. I was terrified for days. When I finally told her, she was not happy, but I guess she figured she wouldn't interfere. Once I told her though, a huge weight was lifted from my shoulders. I could breathe. It took weeks before I could tell her. I think part of me wanted to be too far along for her to talk me into ending it.

When I held my baby girl in my arms, I finally understood love. I stopped seeking it from men who only wanted one thing. I stopped seeking approval from others, because I finally had it. What I learned later on though, was that all along, God had loved me. Through all my reckless behavior, He kept me.

Now, twelve years later, I am trying to be an example for my daughter. She's entering that age where she is curious about everything and I know that temptations will come. I pray that I've given her enough information, been open enough for her to talk to, and easy enough to approach. My mother wasn't those things. If I'm honest though, I can't say for sure I would have talked to her about my decision to start having sex, even if she had been. My mother and grandmother were both very closed-mouthed about certain subjects. The talk about puberty went like this, "You can get pregnant now. Don't bring no babies in here!"

So, hopefully being open with my daughter and thoroughly educating her on what's going on with her body will help.

In hindsight, I don't know what I would have done if I'd had a baby at eighteen. Maybe I would have finished college sooner. One thing that did happen when I decided to go forth with my second pregnancy was that I knew I had to finish school. My daughter was the driving force for me to get it done. Perhaps, I'd be in a different career now. I mourned the loss of that baby from the minute I left that abortion clinic until sometime after I was 37 years old when I decided that I am not my past. I forgave myself because God already had when I first asked Him to do so many years before. I always wondered why I did not just stand up to my mother but then I think, maybe she knew best after all. For so long, I held it against her, but I forgave her long before I forgave myself. But I learned that I simply was not ready. Though I hate one life had to end for me to understand that, I'm grateful to have been given a second chance at motherhood. And right now, I'm doing the very best that I can each and every day.

Kay Alizeti is a Georgia native living in the Atlanta metropolitan area. She and her daughter are hungry for words and enjoy reading, dancing and singing. She loves being an example for her daughter and makes certain to stay connected. Kay can be reached online at Twitter— @KayAlizeti and Facebook

Diary of a Modernized Mother

By Yolanda D. Gautier

I believe most women possess a motherly instinct, regardless of whether it is manifested in their own biological offspring, or exhibited in their nurturing of others.

For me, motherhood has brought me the greatest joy, and some of my deepest pain. I knew from an early age that I wanted to be a mother. My nurturing spirit was demonstrated in everything from the countless animals I "adopted" as a little girl, to my sometimes over-bearing "mothering" of my younger brother. While my aspirations included being an independent, college-degreed woman with a successful career, I also wanted a loving husband and two children to complete my concept of an ideal life experience. Well, I was blessed to have a daughter and a son (and thankfully not both at the same time), and a supportive spouse to help me raise them. Yet, even with my predisposition for taking care of others, nothing fully prepared me for the wide range of emotions that I have encountered in my journey through motherhood.

From my daughter being born two months early, to my son arriving a week late, I experienced the joy and the pain of bringing forth life through the miracle of childbirth. Even before making their grand entrances into the world, my children presented me with many changes and challenges. I will never forget the overwhelming sensation of that first unmistakable flutter of life in my womb, along with the relentless morning, afternoon and evening sickness that I endured in the first few months of pregnancy. I can still recall the food cravings and the food aversions, the joyful anticipation of seeing your child's face for the first time, and the fearful apprehension as the due date drew near. You know how some women have a "cute" pregnancy…nothing different except a big belly? Well, that definitely wasn't the case for me. Once my children began their life's journey, they completely overtook my body for the time they needed it. It seemed like everything expanded…from my nose to my stomach, my hips, and my feet. And why was it that at night, as soon as I got comfortably nestled within numerous pads and pillows, that my bladder decided it was time to be emptied? Sometimes pregnancy seemed more like a cruel joke than a blessed event.

While pregnant with my daughter, I had a condition called "pre-eclampsia," which made my first motherhood experience a risky one. This condition caused me to have a dangerously elevated blood pressure, which caused a lot of weight gain and fluid retention. By the time my doctor had ordered me to bedrest for the remainder of my pregnancy,

I looked about ready to "pop," although I still had a few months to go. Even though I understood the gravity of my condition, my only concern was for the health and safety of my yet unborn child.

While I am a pretty active person by nature, I resolved myself to follow the doctor's orders, but only had about a week to do so. At 32 weeks of pregnancy, my condition took a turn for the worse. As a result, I had to undergo an emergency cesarean section surgery to save my daughter... and myself. While in a haze of medications and mayhem, my ears were only attuned for one sound, which was my daughter's first feeble cry.

I was only given a brief moment to see her before she was whisked away to the neonatal intensive care unit of the hospital. While she was being delivered, they discovered a tear in my placenta that was preventing her from getting what she needed to develop normally. As a result, she was literally "starving" in my womb, and at 32 weeks gestation, only weighed two pounds and eleven ounces at birth. While I endured the pain of recovery from surgery, and separation from my newborn child, Bryanna fought for her life, and after five long weeks was strong enough to come home, and without any complications...God is good.

Well, about five years later, I had enough of a memory lapse from the first experience to try my hand at motherhood again. This time, my son took his own sweet time to arrive. Since my first pregnancy was considered a "high-risk," I took all of the necessary precautions in order to better my chances at a healthy pregnancy. I really wanted to have a normal pregnancy experience. I remember feeling a little uncomfortable being the only mother in my Lamaze class that had already given birth, but I was determined not to miss out on anything the second time around.

While I was in the midst of enduring what seemed to be the hottest Houston summer ever, my son decided to wait until about a week after his due date to make his appearance. In fact, I had already scheduled a labor inducement for the following Monday. With two days left to go, my water finally broke. I remember at the time I was at home completely absorbed in a television performance by Maxwell, who was my favorite singer at the time, and reluctantly left the room for what I thought was yet another one of my countless trips to the bathroom. I soon realized this was not a test, as the contractions came fast and furiously. My husband rushed me to the hospital, only to discover that I had not even dilated yet, and so began a long evening of waiting.

First, I was given medication to slow down the contractions, then another one later to speed them up. After a few rounds of more painful contractions (and forgetting everything I learned in Lamaze class), it was determined that I could not deliver safely without another caesarean section. Although I was disappointed that all of my efforts had yielded a similar outcome, I was also relieved that I did not have to continue the exhausting process of labor. I decided I had enough of the "full experience." Unlike my firstborn, Evan weighed in at a healthy eight pounds and seven ounces, and boldly announced his arrival with a strong cry and wide-eyed observation.

Finally, I experienced the pleasure of holding my newborn at my chest, as we briefly bonded, before he was taken away for the routine procedures.

The next several years of motherhood involved a whirlwind of milestones and emotions, including sleepless nights, inconsolable crying, teething, unsolicited advice (good and bad), childhood illnesses, temper tantrums, separation anxiety (on both parts), rebellious natures, sibling rivalry and silent treatments. I remember moments when the children that I had "brought into this world," made me seriously consider wanting to "take them back out."

On the other hand, the formative years of childrearing were also filled with comfort, hugs, kisses, laughter, joy, pride, accomplishments, fond memories, blessings, peace and most of all…love.

As a mother, I have honed my skills as a cook, a maid, a doctor, a detective, a tutor, a mediator, a secretary, a counselor and a banker, all while trying to maintain a healthy balance in my marriage and my career.

Raising children in a time where technological advances have literally put the "world at our fingertips" has presented new challenges that my parents, and parents before them, did not have to deal with. There was a time when parents could more easily protect their children from bad influences by controlling what they watched on television, what they listened to on the radio, and who they associated with.

Now, our efforts are constantly challenged by a barrage of information that is easily accessible to them through the Internet, and the wider acceptance of negative language and images on public media outlets, that would have been more highly censored a few years ago. Don't even get me started on cell phones. My husband and I decided that our children did not need their own cell phones until they became teenagers, and even then, it was more as a means to stay in contact with them during the day, rather than succumbing to social pressures.

Of course, it seemed like whenever we tried to call them, their cell phones would mysteriously refuse to work properly, or they couldn't hear it ringing ... or vibrating. Now there is a whole sub-culture of text messaging, complete with its own language, that I am struggling to keep up with, in order to effectively communicate with my children. (You see, actually dialing a number and having a conversation with someone is so "taboo" nowadays.) However, all was not lost in the onslaught of technological advancement. When they asked, "Mom, how do you spell…?" or "How do you solve this math problem?" I calmly replied, "Go look it up on the Internet... you look up everything else!"

Then, I proceeded to remind them of how when I was growing up we had to actually use a dictionary or an encyclopedia to look for information, and that would usually be the end of it.

As a "Millennium Mom," I have walked the fine line between being the "old school" disciplinarian, and being "the cool mom". I am still young enough to remember my childhood eagerness to "be grown," and yet old enough to realize that you should take your time to enjoy life before having to navigate the responsibilities of adulthood. My daughter is now a mature young adult, who is currently seeking her college degree in her chosen career path, while my son is a budding musician, who is enjoying the full experience of his teenager years. Although, my love and "mother lion" protectiveness for my children has not diminished over the years, I am now in the process of learning the art of letting go, while continuing to be a source of safety, guidance and instruction.

There is so much more that I want to do and say to prepare my children for their life's journey, but at the same time, I am actually beginning to look forward to getting back to myself. For all of the selfless sacrifices of motherhood, I have learned that you must take time to replenish yourself, in order to been able to give to others what they need from you. I want my children to know that no matter how successful or independent they may become, as their mother, I will always see that bright-eyed baby that once depended upon me for everything, and will continue to love and protect them as fiercely as I am able.

Yolanda D. Gautier is a native of Houston, Texas, and a proud graduate of Xavier University of Louisiana, with a B.S. in Finance. She is currently an insurance industry professional, and an active member of Alpha Kappa Alpha Sorority, Inc., who resides in the Houston area with her husband Byron and their children. She is a self-published author of two novels available at http://www.lulu.com/spotlight/ydgautier.

Diary of a Reading Mom

By Kimyatta Walker

I've always liked to help people learn things. For as long as I can remember, if I knew it, so did everyone else. So naturally, when I found out I was expecting, I went into overdrive trying to find ways to help my unborn baby learn. I read everything I could get my hands on that told me ways to make my baby intelligent. I prayed diligently to God, "Lord, please let my baby be intelligent, teachable and have a love for words and music."

I would sing to my baby each day. I chose six songs that I thought conveyed how I felt about my baby and sang them in succession. I had also read that I should read to her and talk to her as often as I could each day. I just knew I'd have the smartest baby there ever was.

Well, once she was born, I discovered that some of what I believed was true. The same songs that I sang during my pregnancy calmed her when she was a baby. She would always stare at me with these big beautiful eyes and I knew I was appreciated. When she was just under two years old, when she'd get fussy and I'd grab her into an embrace to sing to her, if I started with the first song, she would grab my lips with her little fingers and pinch them together. I guess she knew that meant sleepy time.

One of the songs was from the opening sequence of the movie, *Prince of Egypt*. She was four years old before she could make it through the beginning of that movie. Even now, when I sing to her, she covers her ears and shakes her head while making lots of noise. I'm sure she does that because on some level, my singing voice still calms her. It has absolutely nothing to do with the fact that I sing like some of those people who don't make it on *American Idol.*

Each night, I would read to her before bedtime. I pointed to the words and as she was able, I let her point with me. I grew more and more excited as we read each night because I thought I was growing a little reader. To aid in the development of her literacy skills, I labeled everything in her bedroom and when we watched television or movies, I would turn on the closed captioning or subtitles. It drove everyone else crazy but I didn't care, I was building life skills for her.

One day, when she was about three years old, my daughter or "The Girl," as I call her, was standing in front of the television, as was her custom, watching the words go across the screen. I was half watching, half reading. Suddenly, she shouted, "Go back! I saw ass!"

Er? I was a little torn, because, I thought I heard my three-year-old daughter say a cuss word. On the other hand, she had read a word! Of all the words to read and recognize first, she chose a forbidden one. So, the excited-me obliged her and went back so that she could see the word. I high-fived her to let her know that it was correct, but I let her know that was a not a word little girls should say. My dear intelligent daughter just laughed and kept watching the play and laughing at the antics on stage. That was the last time we watched one of those. Good message in the play, but after that, everything we watched was rated G.

Of course, when she got to kindergarten, she never had trouble with blends. But she was always the one to come up with the –ass words.

I learned that my budding reader was not only learning to read bad words, but she was learning to say them, too. Now, I don't cuss, nor does my mother…but my grandmother... well, she's my grandmother...and she says what she wants. She gives the occasional "uh oh" when my daughter's around. Well, imagine my surprise when again, I heard my three-year-old utter other words that she'd seen via closed captioning. She had finished her first year of dance and we went to Wendy's for a celebratory lunch. She climbed up in the chair and started taking things out of her kid's meal bag. She pulled everything out and got to the surprise, looked at in disgust and said, "What the hell is this?" just as calm as though it was completely normal. Again, I was mortified! My sister on the other hand was so tickled that she had to just get up and walk away. I learned that I had to be super careful about what printed words I was exposing her to.

Before long, when we read, I would stop at a word and she would point to it and say what it was. Now, of course, I knew she wasn't really reading, but certain words, depending on the story, she could show me. She knew the stories. The day she took Eric Carle's *Brown Bear, Brown Bear* from me to "read" it to me I was thrilled! She loved that book and we read it each night.

When she entered kindergarten, she was four years old for a few days because of her early birth date. Her teacher was so impressed with her literary skills and told me that she never would have guessed that my daughter was one of the younger kids in her class. She complimented my daughter's maturity, and intellectual prowess. I, of course, beamed. I thought my prayers and all the hard work I did during my pregnancy and in her early years had paid off! She was really an academic star. When she took the developmental reading assessment in kindergarten toward the end of the year, her scores were out of the water. In kindergarten, she needed a score higher than three to be considered ready for first grade. At the end of first grade you need a 14 and it goes up with each grade level. Well, my sugar bean scored a 96. That was a high school reading level. So, here I was thinking *Yay! I did something right!* It was a big thing for a kindergarten student to make such a score. We were ecstatic.

All that reading preparation and excitement about words and I just knew I'd birthed a reader. She would be just like me in every way. I imagined us spending hours at the library and book store, perusing the book shelves trying to find the latest and greatest reads. Boy was I wrong! While my daughter *could* read and read well, she did not like to read at all! *Gasp*! Certainly, this was a mistake. *Really God?* That's not funny.

In elementary school, they had incentives for reading. They got accelerated reader points for which they could trade for prizes. The Girl would get a book from the library but kept finding books that were easy, so that she could get points in a hurry. She never wanted to pick a book that would challenge her. I was so angry when her teacher told me what she was doing. Now, surely, I knew no book on a ninth grade level would really interest her but she was ready for something more than the books with fifteen words in the entire book. Of course, I had to fix this. This was my reader! She had to like to read. So, I went and found every princess book I could find and forced them on her. Why was I torturing myself? I've tried offering incentives for reading. We would fill out a form and she could get free tokens at Chuck E. Cheese. That only lasted for so long. Now, what incentive is there? ITunes gift cards? A phone? Umm..I think not!

For years though, I would try to find books that I thought might interest her and make her read them. My attitude was "Gosh darn it, doo hickey to heck you are gonna read and you are gonna like it!"

It has yet to work that way.

Now, a seventh grader, The Girl has taken to reading like a snowflake takes to a flame. She acts like it is pure torture to do her required reading each afternoon. She is dying to get on Instagram. Since she rarely has homework that she brings home (usually she does it at school), I have given her an hour of required reading each afternoon. She can read whatever she'd like to read, but I once found out that she was not reading at all. According to her, "I didn't want to read the next book because I wanted to wait until the movie came out next year."

Now she knew that wouldn't fly. That night, we marched to the library and I found some books she might like and let her choose three of them to read at home.

There were some popular series books that she liked, but I guess she got bored with the series because she stopped wanting them. I think maybe she just outgrew it…but I am determined that she *needs* to read and learn to enjoy it.

Recently, I found a book by one of my favorite authors, who writes a teen series, that she seems to like. This is how I knew I was winning finally. I was working and I heard her yelling in what seemed to be a heated conversation. Then I heard her say, "No this <mumble> didn't!"

I'm not sure what she mumbled, but given her history, I'm sure it's a word she shouldn't have said. When I paused a moment in my work to ask what was wrong, she started telling me about a character's mother. I tried not to be overly excited. I didn't want to scare her. I just nodded and went back to work. The next day, I asked a question and she answered flippantly. Then she said, that's what Maya would have said. (Maya is a character from her book). We have never had a conversation about a book that she read except that first one with Katniss Everdeen. That was two years ago.

I told her she couldn't watch the movie until she read the book. Now though, I think she might be on to something else. This Maya character might be just what she needs. Now, if only Instagram had book passages as photos…maybe we'd be on to something. Either that, or Maya needs an Instagram account.

Ah, well. I'll take what I can get. Perhaps this is just what she needed. We shall see.

Kimyatta Walker is the mother of a feisty preteen. She and her daughter live just outside of the metropolitan Atlanta area where they are learning the joys of being mother and daughter. Kimyatta can be found on the web at www.kimyattawrites.com.

Diary of a Telecommuting Mom

By Kimberly Holley Clark

Dear Diary,

Like most children of the 70's and 80's, I grew up watching my maternal caregivers toiling day and night to provide a safe and comfortable environment for their families. And for the most part, the work they performed included duties both inside and outside of the home.

While I did not witness it firsthand, I've been regaled, a million times, with tales about the laborious domestic work my beloved grandmother had to do to help support her family in the 1940's and early 1950's. After cooking and cleaning another household all day, she would have to come home and, without any assistance from the modern-day conveniences we are afforded today, or a well-stocked neighborhood store, prepare a nutritious and budget conscious meal that would sufficiently feed her own family of seven.

As a young child, I watched my own mother leave the house at the crack of dawn and often not return until well after the dinner hour. Even though she was dead tired from working as a warehouse worker at Sears and Roebuck and then later as a letter carrier for the Post Office, she still managed to prepare a hearty dinner for my sister, brothers and me, when she got home from her shift.

When I was a teenager, life circumstances necessitated that I move in with my mother's sister. In my opinion, she may have had the hardest job of all. No, I'm not referring to the taxing task of rearing a teenage me, whereas I must admit that was no walk in the park. I was actually alluding to the fact that she was employed in, what I believe to be, the most stressful, tedious and underappreciated profession there is—teaching.

When I went to live with her, she already had 13 years of experience under her belt. She taught seventh grade Texas History and continued teaching it for another 15 years; until she retired early to care for my ailing grandmother. As a member of my aunt's household, I poignantly witnessed her driving more than 40 miles, one-way, just to get to the middle school she taught at. What's more, her workday was rarely over when she stepped through the door late in the evening; because she still had papers that had to be graded and lesson plans to prepare.

Yeah, my maternal caregivers certainly instilled in me a strong work ethic. While I was growing up, they most definitely patterned behaviors, which taught me that mere survival in this world frequently requires hard work and from time to time mandates that one put in long arduous hours just to get the job done. Now if you want to get ahead in life, that's an entirely different story. In that case, I learned you have to double up on your efforts and work twice as hard and long. Trust me when I say, through blood, sweat and tears I took all those life lessons to heart. Between you and me, though, I think I might have a rather difficult time convincing my children that I did.

Although writing is my true passion, I do have what is commonly referred to as a "day job" and for the foreseeable future, I plan on keeping said job. That is until I make it big in the publishing world. In the meantime, however, I have been very blessed with a flexible schedule and the ability to telecommute several days a week. Man, I love technology!

To facilitate my telecommuting, I have a fully functioning home office, equipped with a fax machine, printer, scanner, and a high speed Wi-Fi connection. And of course, I have my trusty laptop. Yes, my office, at home, provides me with everything I need to excel at my job. But truth be told, I can often be found sitting at the kitchen table, perched on the sofa, or worst, propped up in the bed, while performing my daily tasks. I think I should pause and reiterate that I know how extremely blessed I am. Trust me when I tell you, I do not take my great fortune for granted. Just ask my manager, or any of my clients, my work and the quality of the products I support have not suffered one bit since I stopped driving to the office every day.

I was actually one of the early pioneers of telecommuting at my company. As a matter of fact, I have been doing it now for going on 10 years. As such, my children have no real recollection of me ever working any other schedule. You know the hectic one that had me up at the crack of dawn struggling to get two babies, then toddlers, afterward preschoolers, and eventually small children ready for daycare and school by 6:30 a.m., all so I could be at work by 7:45 a.m. They have absolutely no memories of me coming home exhausted and frustrated after working a nine hour day, under a micromanaging boss, and then having to navigate Houston's habitually gridlocked traffic to get home; but not able to go directly to bed, because I had to cook dinner and then help them with their homework, before getting them ready for bed. That is if we made it that far. More often than not, we simply conked out before getting an opportunity to perform any semblance of a bedtime ritual.

As idyllic as my work scenario may seem, there is a downside to it. From the outside looking in, it may appear as if I simply sit around the house and play on the computer all day. Since this is the image of me that is foremost in my kid's minds, I'm worried that they may have concluded that making a living is a piece of cake. Well, at least one of them might feel that way. You see, my sixteen-year-old son has yet to enter the workforce. My twenty-year-old daughter, on the other hand, has had the opportunity to punch the proverbial clock.

When she was in high school, my daughter worked for about nine months, at one of the local grocery stores. Apparently, she got tired of me saying I wasn't made of money whenever she asked for some. From what I've gathered, her brief brush with employment taught her how to work with a diverse group of people, to be timely, and to submit to the authority of a sometimes incompetent supervisor. It also taught her that she did not want to do that for the rest of her life; so she quit and devoted her senior year to her studies and extracurricular activities. Her efforts ultimately paid off. She was accepted to one of the top schools in our state, which just happens to be my alma mater, and for the last three years she has been following in her mother's footsteps by pursuing a degree in Chemical Engineering. A degree plan that has led to summer internships at two of the world's largest refining companies. Obviously my unorthodox working style has not impeded her ability to secure gainful employment.

On the contrary, my poor son remains blissfully unaware of the rigors of the workplace; although he seems quite eager to get a job. Unfortunately, his schedule is jam-packed with school and extracurricular activities; consequently, there is little to no room for him to fit in a part-time job. Of course, that doesn't stop him from asking any and everyone he meets, if he can work for them. While I admire his tenacity, I hope he doesn't become disillusioned with working once he lands a job and finds out that it often involves putting in hard work and long hours for very little pay, especially in those entry level positions. I hope he realizes that you have to pay your dues first to prove that you are worthy of a position that allows you to set your own hours and work independently of the group or an imposing supervisor.

In this world of TiVo, DVR's and video on demand, I get the sense that more and more young people are seeking immediate gratification and not just in their entertainment. Many of them are seeking the same instantaneous fulfillment in their careers. They want to graduate from college and immediately start living the same cushy lifestyles as their parents. Even though I make it look extremely easy, I constantly remind my kids that no one handed me a telecommuting job on a silver platter. I had to methodically plan and bargain for it, forgoing raises and promotions in the process. All so I could have a harmonious work-life balance. Growing up as a latchkey kid, I really wanted to be home with my children if and when they needed me, but my household's finances required that I maintain a full-time job. Fortunately, the good Lord saw fit to bless me with a position that would essentially allow me to do both, but I hope my good fortune does not become my children's curse.

The preliminary results are promising. My daughter seems to be on the right track and my son talks a good game. However, only the future will tell if they've learned to do as I say as opposed to what they actually *perceive* me doing. Yes, time will reveal whether my unconventional work schedule has negatively impacted my children. It is my sincerest hope that the work ethic that I have instilled in them will be strong enough to prepare them for tomorrow's ever-changing job market. I pray that I have adequately prepared them to pound the pavement, even though I sometimes keep my pajamas on all day.

Kimberly Holley-Clark is a married mother of two and stepmother to one. She enjoys spending time with her husband, of nearly 20 years, children and numerous friends. Kim is also a prolific and trade-savvy freelance copywriter for various ezines and websites. In addition, she is a regular contributor to the award winning Think Act Parent Black parenting blog. Visit her online at www.lulu.com/kimberlyclark.

Diary of a Renaissance Mom

By Kristen Wright-Matthews

I gave birth to my son on Monday, August 27, 2007. A couple of hours into my labor, I was rushed into the delivery room. My blood pressure had risen and my baby's heartbeat had stopped. Once they removed him from my body, the nurse held him over my face quickly and then she ran off. My doctor then said in a crackling voice, "Kristen, he is not breathing well and we have to put him on oxygen."

I thought I would die. The baby boy that I wanted so much was in jeopardy. I was taken into recovery, where I cried desperately for hours until finally my doctor came in to tell me that my son was doing fine. He had been on 100 percent oxygen for the first five hours of his life. While he was literally having life pumped into him, I was dying inside. It was the longest five hours of my life, and if the outcome had been any different, well, I just don't know.

It was a long few days in the hospital because I was unable to hold my baby due to the tubes they had him connected to. It wasn't until the third day that I was able hold him (and the tubes) to feed him. Unfortunately, that was the day that I was slated to be released and my baby had to stay for two more days. I was there every three hours on the hour to feed him until he was released. Ironically, we had moved into the area of the hospital just two months before his birth, but truth be told, if I had to drive 100 miles and back, it would have been no problem. The way that I felt with him in my arms was unlike anything else I had ever experienced.

On the fifth day, my baby was allowed to come home. It was Saturday, September 1 (my daddy's birthday) and my older sister had flown in just in time to pick him up from the hospital. Because he had been in ICU, this would be the first day that I was really able to bond with my new baby boy, holding him closely with no tubes attached. He was beautiful. I promised him that I would never leave his side.

My last six and a half years have been a blur in terms of my career and life outside of my family. Many first-time mothers are guilty of this, I'm sure. I am the first to say that I laid the young, fun-loving, aggressive, popular, business-savvy woman that I worked so hard to become to rest on the day I gave birth to my son. When I saw that sweet little face, and then I almost lost him, something came over me. I was no longer Kristen, but C.J.'s mom.

I immediately lost interest in going out, socializing with friends who weren't moms, and gained a serious affection for mommy-and-me events, children's books, and anything else that would help in the development of my son's physical, mental, emotional, and even academic development. I was a monster!

I can proudly say that my husband and I have done a great job so far in terms of raising a smart, well-rounded boy. He has a laundry list of interests and talents; a schedule as tight as the President; and I have been reduced to driver, cook, and assistant— a title he has affectionately called me on occasion. He runs track, plays soccer and football, and is a member of the Cub Scouts. Additionally, he has his own program called Blankies 4 My Buddies, in which we collect blankets to distribute to sick and displaced kids during the cold months. This landed him on the front page of the local newspaper last December. He is really a phenomenal kid, but he definitely has his flaws.

New millennium kids are different. My son is stubborn and wants to do things when he wants to do them. He is manipulative and knows how to change the direction of a conversation. He is very independent. On top of that, he thinks everything is funny.

My attitude today and the attitude my mother would have taken back in the 70's when I was growing up are at opposite ends of the spectrum. My head would have literally rolled if I had the gall to say some of the things that my son does. On most days, I have to remind myself how I felt when they snatched him away from me on the night he was born. He is very outspoken like I was, but I knew when to stop. When my mom said no, I didn't keep asking why. And I especially wouldn't take my chances in trying her.

I can say so much about my boy. He thinks he is smart enough and strong enough, and can handle any situation he is confronted with. If it's something that he really wants to do, he will try it at all costs…even if he knows that a punishment will follow. That's when the manipulation and joking starts. Everyone who knows him or follows our social media constantly says that he needs to be on television. Whether it's something funny he said or did, or his comedic dance moves, he really knows how to capture your attention and heart. He is a charismatic kid, and will not sacrifice his passion for fun and being happy for anyone or anything. Ultimately, I guess like any other six-year-old boy, he just wants to have fun. As long as he knows there are consequences, I guess we're doing our job. But, as a mother of "little danger dude," at times, it can be a little scary.

Just last year, I was a broken woman. On June 11, 2013, I gave birth to a daughter, Karsen Angelica. I was only five months pregnant. I developed an infection around my water bag and started to dilate prematurely. Unfortunately, at only a mere .6 ounces, she had not developed enough to survive. This now was the most devastating thing that I have ever endured, and believe me I have experienced some tragedy in my life. My husband and I made a decision to cremate our daughter, and we carry her memory with us each and every day. During this time of grief and healing, C.J. has showed so much love and compassion for his lost sister until it is amazing. It is the one and only thing that I've ever known to make him sad.

The loss of Karsen and the life of C.J. reminded me that I have to live. Because just like one day my sweet little girl was fluttering around in my belly and the next day she was gone—that's how life is. You have to make the most of each day and do the things you love. I once had a passion for writing, public speaking, practicing PR, helping people to make their dreams a reality, volunteering, teaching and being a role model for young people. These things once kept me alive. They kept me relevant. They kept me fulfilled. These passions burned within me and radiated outwardly, attracting so many wonderful people and situations toward me. I missed that so when God placed it on my heart just a few months ago to start writing again, I did. It was that day that I learned about this opportunity to enter a diary submission to The Motherhood Diaries 2, and here I am. I made the decision to LIVE like C.J., and not to let Karsen's death be in vain.

On January 1, 2014, I decided to take note of C.J.'s outlook and actually learn something from him. If this goes to print, I will hide it until he is a very old man. But seriously, I decided to remove myself from the bondage that I inflicted upon myself to for the past six and a half years. If this six-year-old boy was not willing to compromise his passions, why should I?

My son loves life, and he has truly inspired me to find myself again—and step back into my purpose. His happy spirit and determination to succeed in everything he does reminded me of who I was—who I am. He has made me realize that I am not only C.J.'s mom or Chris' wife, but I am Kristen Wright-Matthews, a writer, a publicist, a strong and passionate woman, who is *also* a proud wife and mother.

Although only nine months ago, moving on was the last thing I wanted to hear, but now I truly believe that things happen for a reason. I'm so glad that when I laid my passions to rest, I did not bury them. If you're a mom, and you have goals and desires, go for it! You are a mother, but you are also a beautiful, strong, and worthy being that was individually created by God. You deserve everything that He has created you to be. God gives us talents and gifts to use and to share. If you do not share your gifts, you may not only be hurting yourself, but you may be blocking someone else's blessing, thus not abiding by the good Lord's Word.

Isn't it profound that I learned this lesson from my children?

Kristen Wright-Matthews is a publicist and writer from Los Angeles. She currently resides in Awendaw, SC with her husband Chris, son C.J., and parents, Mr. & Mrs. Ronald and Jane Wright. She can be reached at www.hustlemomchronicles.com or via email at hustlemomchronicles@gmail.com.

www.ingramcontent.com/pod-product-compliance
Lightning Source LLC
Chambersburg PA
CBHW051822040426
42447CB00006B/328

* 9 7 8 1 6 2 5 1 7 4 5 2 9 *